About the Author

Sarah Ivens, PhD, is the best-selling author of nine lifestyle and wellness books, including *A Modern Girl's Guide to Getting Hitched* and *Forest Therapy: Seasonal Ways to Embrace Nature for a Happier You*. She is the founding Editor in Chief of *OK!* magazine in the US, and is a regular contributor to the *Daily Mail*, the *Telegraph*, *Stella*, *Glamour*, *Marie Claire*, the *New York Post* and *YOU* magazine, amongst others. She was also the editor of *Mother, Other: Words by Women on Bereavement*

A Londoner turned Southern Belle, she now splits her time between Austin, Texas and England, having previously spent five years in New York, where she ran *OK!*, and two years in Los Angeles, where she worked for the drama development team at HBO and certified as a life coach.

Sarah holds a PhD in Comparative Humanities from the University of Louisville, Kentucky, her work focusing on the changes and choices faced by mothers since the 1950s, and how the ideas of home and homeland shape a woman's life.

Sarah's other books include

A Modern Girl's Guide to Dynamic Dating

A Modern Girl's Guide to Etiquette

A Modern Girl's Guide to the Perfect Single Life

A Modern Girl's Guide to Getting Organized

A Modern Girl's Guide to Networking

The Bride's Guide to Unique Weddings

*No Regrets: 101 Fabulous Things to Do Before
You're Too Old, Married or Pregnant*

The Zen Mama

SARAH IVENS

piatkus

PIATKUS

First published in Great Britain in 2020 by Piatkus

1 3 5 7 9 10 8 6 4 2

A CIP catalogue record for this book
is available from the British Library.

Note: the names of the people who have provided their
stories have been changed to protect their privacy.

ISBN 978-0-349-42335-7

Typeset in Swift by M Rules
Printed and bound in Great Britain by
Clays Ltd, Elcograph S.p.A

Papers used by Piatkus are from well-managed forests
and other responsible sources.

Piatkus
An imprint of
Little, Brown Book Group
Carmelite House
50 Victoria Embankment
London EC4Y 0DZ

An Hachette UK Company
www.hachette.co.uk

www.improvementzone.co.uk

For my mother, Helen, who has always done everything she can to make my brothers and me feel happy and secure, even when life has left her unhappy or insecure. Mum, your bravery and kindness are inspiring.

Contents

Introduction   1

1   Get Comfortable with Your New Identity   13
2   Give Up the Guilt   35
3   Choose Freedom   55
4   Learn to Love Your Body   75
5   Understand Your Mama Brain   97
6   Create a Serene Home   119
7   Find Your Tribe   139
8   Set Your Own Expectations   159
9   Make Peace with Your Critics   177
10   Follow Your Unique Path to Happiness   195

Epilogue – Peace Out   217
Further Reading   219
Acknowledgements   225

Introduction

A few months ago, two girlfriends and I met for a long-overdue dinner in a quiet restaurant equidistant from our homes. We were not the large, rambunctious group that we were supposed to be. One friend had texted in the morning to say that her husband had a last-minute work dinner, which took priority, and it was too late to find a babysitter. Another had called at 6pm, as I was pulling my tired bones into something vaguely stylish while rush-feeding my children chicken nuggets and broccoli, to say that she was just leaving the doctor's, her son had a virus and she didn't feel that she could leave him with his dad, who panicked when the kids were ill. A third friend, battling chronic pain while looking after an elderly father-in-law, was an expected no-show; she found it harder and harder to make time for herself outside of her two daughters, her husband's family, and work.

'The trouble is,' my friend Jenny said, as we delved into a stack of sweet potato fries and the oft-frequented topic of motherhood guilt and the quest to 'have it all', 'we expect women to raise children as if they don't work and expect them to work as if they don't have children.' The key word – the one that has always set off my alarm bells – was 'expect'. Mothering was all about *expectations*, and often not our own. 'Can I be controversial and suggest things were easier when gender roles were established and limits set,' Jenny continued, 'instead of now, when we're expected to have fulfilling careers, tiny waists, friendships worthy of an episode of *Sex and The City*, and be everything and more to our children – and partners!'

'Not possible,' Michelle volunteered. 'Motherhood has made me anxious.'

'It will if we try to maintain these *expectations* that we'll be good at everything,' I agreed. 'But I refuse to. I'm a terrible cook, I don't own an iron, I have never been to a SoulCycle class, but I know what's important to me and my family. Everything else I've let slide into a ditch. A ditch which, admittedly, might reek of shame, guilt and failure to other people.'

'What do you do about the harmful wafts of shame, guilt and fear of failure?' Jenny asked.

'I hold my nose,' I joked, shuddering at the thought of the first few years of my parenting journey when I'd spend sleepless nights worried about how I was possibly damaging my children and what other people thought of me, 'and plough through until I get to the sweet, sweet pastures of mind your own business.'

This conversation, or something similar, is one I've heard a million times in my nearly eight years of being a mother, and one that is played out every day, in every way, as modern mothers struggle to find balance and confidence in their new and arguably most-important role. Overwhelming? Yes, because the immeasurable love affair that will begin when you become a mother will be life-affirming and beautiful, but along with your bundle of joy the stork will dump at your feet bags of despair, guilt, frustration, fear, total lack of alone time and a fierier relationship with your partner. And as these bundles of joy get bigger and bigger, more and more doubts and worries can sneak into your life.

Getting into my groove

Very early on, to stay sane, I knew I had to draw up my own parenting philosophy, one that suited *me and my children* rather than society, or the voices on social media, or mothers from the generations before who were desperate to share their dated advice and opinions loudly with me. I found my Zen when I stopped listening to them and listened to my heart and head.

Zen is a style of Buddhism that originated in China over a thousand years ago. Central to the philosophy of Zen is the practice of meditation, which followers believe will bring about a sense of calm and detachment from the noise of the world around us, and an ability to trust our own intuition. It encourages mindfulness and self-awareness, so practitioners can comprehend their own thoughts and emotions. When someone can understand their true nature, they become awakened. In modern times, the meaning of Zen has become a shortcut for being peaceful and relaxed. This philosophy can help mamas by reminding us of the importance of:

- Being in the moment
- Trusting your instincts
- Silencing critical outside voices, and your own harmful inner voice
- Finding time to relax and be alone
- Dropping illusions and lies, and focusing on your truth
- Contemplating your own route to calmness and contentment

It is this sense of Zen that will inform the next ten chapters. *The Zen Mama* outlines a way of life to create a chilled parent and a chilled child; a guide to letting go of parenting expectations and fears to give you the tools to raise courageous, confident kids. *The*

Zen Mama philosophy is that mother and child complement each other in adventures and experiences, always putting safety first but without getting caught up in the anxieties, drama, impossible expectations and mental baggage that too often comes with modern parenting in this social-media and judgemental age. It is about tuning out the din of other people's decisions and doubts, and trusting your heart, your head and your children. It will offer a few laughs, 'I hear you' moments and a sense of relief to the mothers in the middle, who love their child but need help accepting that their boobs now resemble the bags goldfish come in at the fair; or mothers who need reassurance that they can turn off the cacophony of news headlines and the crowing of competitive mummies and just love their child how their child wants to be loved – mothers who can hear the distant beat of their own drum and who want to find their own rhythm.

I'm not Zen-in-the-mountain-top, mellow-monk sense of Zen, so don't think that becoming a Zen mama is unachievable in your current chaos. I still have moments when I am a fishwife of extreme volume, bellowing at my kids to put on a coat when icicles have formed on their eyebrows, or giving them ferocious side-long looks until they remember their manners. I can be curt, grumpy, snappy, distracted and sometimes as immature as they are. But, through my training as a life coach and my interest in Zen philosophy, and as a parenting journalist and researcher with a PhD focused on motherhood and mothering, I have sought and uncovered many tips to give mothers and their offspring the healthiest emotional bricks to build their lives upon and to make sure that they are asking themselves important questions, not just blindly parenting through fear.

Becoming a Zen mama was a journey for me, but becoming a mama was an even harder one. In my thirties there was nothing I wanted more than to procreate. I started cooing over little ones in coffee shops and even – the shame! – bought a baby-name dictionary to peruse while commuting to and from my office. But, like so many women, fertility was not my friend. Eighteen months of general, casual, non-scary shagging with my husband was fruitless, so our once-romantic sex life became a thing of peeing-on-stick pressure, military-timed ejaculations and blood-curdling headstands. My husband sulked and felt used, I got ratty and glum, but we knew it would all be worth it when we cradled our perfect child in our arms, imagining that a baby would complete me (us) and give us a happy-ever-after. Our journey to parenthood had a few more twists and turns for us, and three miscarriages, which broke our hearts, before we finally got to hold a healthy baby in our arms.

At last, thankfully, William arrived, followed by Matilda two years later. My life must have felt complete, right? I really, really, really wanted to be a mother, so it must have been easy, this transition from *me* to *we*. I must have glowed with contentment, peace and love like a fairy-lit Virgin Mary on Christmas Eve from the start. Well, I didn't, actually. I was shocked to find the contented times wrestling for space among the overwhelming moments of confusion, depression and remorse. I was shocked that motherhood wasn't all lullabies and cuddles. I hadn't antici-pated that loving my children with all my heart would mean that I sometimes forgot to love myself, too. I didn't realise that being a mother would mean that I occasionally stopped being me, and that while parenting would stretch me in some areas, other parts of me would shrivel up and die.

My balance was off for the first year of motherhood: I was over-whelmed by love, fear, tiredness, raging hormones, gigantic boobs and the constant whirr of the food processor, and the judgement I felt from some people around me. And even now, seven years on with children who can dress themselves and will sit and watch *The Great British Bake Off* with me, or go for a forest hike without whining or needing to be carried, I understand the external pressure on me (and all of us) to mother in a certain way, to follow a parenting trend, to compete ferociously with other parents, or to worry over and exaggerate every milestone, growth spurt, change of plan or expedition.

I'll give you a heads-up: you will have to grow a tough skin to step away from all this at first, to rise above it. I get strange looks and weird comments from other mothers on a daily basis about the freedom and fun I have with my kids. The judgement and panic surrounding parenthood is outrageous, especially surrounding subjects such as travel, education and discipline. I have been amazed by the gumption of friends and strangers who have made comments about what I am doing: from my very first week mothering my firstborn, when I took William in his pram to a coffee shop because I needed some fresh air and adult conversation and got shouted at for bringing a newborn outside; to last weekend when I took my kids to a music festival which Paul McCartney was headlining, and people barked at me that I was crazy and irresponsible ('There'll be drunk people there!', 'They won't get to bed until midnight!', 'They might hear swearing!') and that it was a waste of money ('They will hate the crowds!', 'They will not remember it!').

When my son started school, his teacher said to me disdainfully, 'What have you been doing with him? He can't read?' I told her that no, he couldn't, he had just turned five years old, but he'd been to a great pre-school that valued kindness and confidence, and that he could make friends with anyone, travelled easily and could entertain himself in the garden for hours – skills that would carry him through life. The teacher tutted. Other mothers told me that their sons were reading Harry Potter. And I genuinely thought: *Thank goodness I'm focused on my son and not everyone else's son, because all this judgement could make me really [swearword] miserable.* We're stressed out and anxious, and the 'mummy needs a cocktail' culture is doing nothing but masking the long-term damage we're doing to ourselves, our children and society when we go along with turning childhood into an extended job interview.

Was it ever really any different, I wondered as I started research-ing this book? Has social media done this to us, or was it always a mother's lot to worry forever? Have we always lost sleep over our children? Have we ever felt that we're good enough? I asked my 70-year-old mother, Helen, a role model and now a grandmother of five who has been there and done that. 'Oh, I've never, ever felt I've done a good job,' she admits bluntly, 'however, I can say, hand on my heart, I've done the best job I could have. Unfortunately, life has taught me that bad things happen 100 per cent out of the blue, so I'm always slightly tense in case things change, but it also means I'm very, very grateful for the good times, and I am relieved when you kids are happy, healthy and financially solvent. I am, however, very thankful that I raised you and your two brothers without the intrusive glare and airbrushing of the Internet.'

Be careful! Be kind!

Throughout *The Zen Mama*, you'll be reminded that self-care and self-compassion are keys to orienting you to a value-driven Zen-mama life. But what does that mean? Does it sound too selfish when we are told we have to give everything to our children? I asked licensed psychiatrist Marianne Stout of The Anxiety Treatment Center of Austin, my adopted home city in Texas, to define self-care and self-compassion, and why mamas need them more than anyone:

'Self-care is anything that genuinely rejuvenates you and energises you. It's thinking long term instead of short term. Personally, when I am feeling overwhelmed or burnt out I would love to reach for a cookie to feel better in the short term, but I have learned that going for a 20-minute walk outside will give me more energy and make me feel better over a longer period. Self-compassion involves self-kindness, and this is where setting realistic goals comes into play. This is when I need to remind myself not to let the great be the enemy of the good. If a 20-minute walk would make me feel good, then certainly a five-mile run would make me feel even better! But I am much more likely to complete a 20-minute walk (especially when I am feeling overwhelmed or burnt out). Being kind to myself in setting achievable, realistic goals helps me to actually complete them and not to turn to the short-term fix (back to that damn cookie). Our social-media-driven culture sets us mamas up for unattainable perfectionism and comparing ourselves to others. When we can use self-care and self-compassion (another component of which is realising that we *all* struggle and no one is perfect and we are connected in that struggle) we can start to make our goals and values more achievable.'

With the internal pressure we already put on ourselves, like my mother describes, it is crucial to eliminate the external pressures. We need to get better at *not* looking to society or strangers to judge our parenting. Ask yourself questions, ask your children and ask your partner questions, and work out what the best answers are for *you*. Quieten the mad world of Instagram, and the shouting opinion of panellists on television breakfast shows, and carefully craft a guide to the values, goals and standards that you know will make you function happily and healthily. Take a step onto your own path, take a deep breath and meditate on what your children need (what life skills you can give your children to be resilient, strong, honest, caring and courageous) and what they don't.

How this book can help you

The Zen Mama will help you to take your own path. Each chapter will allow you to confront with honesty the changes – good and bad – that becoming a parent brings; for example, good changes:

your tolerance to lack of sleep improves; bad changes: you think it's acceptable to wipe snotty noses on your cardigan. The next ten chapters will raise questions about where you see yourself in the world, and how you want your family to interact with it and each other. They will prove that you can move outside of stereotypes of doting hippy momma or feminist working mother. You can be whatever stops your brain from slipping out of your earholes and your relationships from slipping down the drain – whatever makes your family work.

Learning to become a Zen mama will help you to grow and nurture a Zen kid: a child who isn't afraid to be different, who can say no (or yes!) and who can stand up for himself or his friends, who can travel the world, be happy in his own company, and experiment with new things without being overwhelmed with self-doubt. We need to address modern mothering in a book like *The Zen Mama* because if we feed into these current trends for helicopter, lawnmower, attachment or tiger parenting (described on page 21, if these terms have passed you by), we're not only restricting our child's possibilities and opportunities to expand but we're also turning ourselves into taxi drivers, milk maids, housebound skivvies and worse: our families are becoming stressed and depleted of time, confidence, money and joy, and our children, studies prove, are less likely to stand on their own two feet when they grow up.

The Zen Mama will show you how to keep a child safe in a warm embrace while letting them have freedom to explore. It will be your guide to disentangling the crossed wires in our electronically connected world to be mindful and present with your loved ones and the world around you. It will help you to fight the indoor childhood epidemic of dependence on devices and screens to encourage you to get outside and communicate in a healthy manner. It will help you to reduce drama and remind you to let love rule. Being a Zen mama doesn't mean being laid-back, lazy or laissez-faire about your child's behaviour or your mothering skills. It is about choosing your battles with the end game in sight of sending healthy, happy children out into the world as adults.

Towards the end of each chapter you'll find a checklist for you to confirm your own needs and wants on the topic discussed over the previous pages. I call it your PG (Parental Guidance) rating and it is a place for you to note, score and plan your family's priorities going forward. By writing down your responses to the questions, you can focus on what you want to achieve and how you can go about it in a relaxed and less pressured way.

The Ps:

Purpose What values do you want to create for your family?

Perspective What do you and your family consider important? How are you different, and contentedly so, from others around you?

Presence Are you happy right now? How can you be happier?

And the Gs:

Gratitude What do you, your child and your family have to be thankful for?

Goals What short- and long-term goals do you have for your child and your family?

Going for it How can you make your best mama life happen?

Each chapter will conclude with a meditation called 'Take a deep breath, mama': a little burst of optimism to remind you you're not alone. Meditations are frequently used to clear the mind, but they can also be used powerfully, as I do in this book, to give us something positive to contemplate or visualise. This isn't easy, but you can do it.

If this all sounds too hippy woo-woo and idealistic, don't fear – The Zen Mama is clear and concise, full of facts and actionable ideas. Do not for a minute think that this book will be a flippant denial of how hard mothering is; it is the hardest job in the world, at times it feels thankless, monotonous, frustrating, mind-boggling and exhausting. And, of course, there is no true measurement of how successful you are as a parent. When can we judge? When our kids graduate? Or when they get a job? Or when they finally stop seeing the therapist they say you have created the need for? Or rather, I should say, there is no external measurement of success. But this book will be about combining the heart and the head with what works for you and your family, not comparing yourself to others or meeting a societal standard, but being able to look in the mirror each night and saying, 'I did my best.'

The book will support and nurture your journey as a mother like a wise and sympathetic friend (who likes their friend's child), and who, when asked to, suggests ideas and offers her experience rather than sharing her prejudices or punishments. This book is a friend who has every faith in your ability to grow a resilient, creative, caring and smart child – and survive the journey.

Finding my own voice and values in this confusing, judgemental world of motherhood has had a chill-out effect that's been good for my sanity, my marriage, my social life and my kids' future. I am not always a cool character, relaxed and quiet. I am not Zen in a tranquil, silent manner. I am my own version of Zen.

I am Zen because I know what is important to my family and what is not important to my family.

I am Zen because I know what my purpose as a parent is and what my family's shared goals are.

I am Zen because in accepting the monotony, I have achieved a sense of wonder as a mother.

Now let's start taking steps along your particular path to Zen.

1

Get Comfortable with Your New Identity

'Once upon a time there was a mother who, in order to become
a mother, had agreed to change her name'

Salman Rushdie, Midnight's Children

It is a truth universally acknowledged that a good woman in
possession of a small child must be in want of some balance. But
motherhood makes balance harder to come by than a shirtless
romantic hero with his own country estate – and it's not as sexy.
When a little person arrives and your pre-child sense of identity,
your priorities and your routine are placed on a wobbly footing, it's
easy to fall prey to insecurity and self-doubt. Who am I again? Who
do I want to be?

When, as a new mother, you can no longer be the carefree dom-
inatrix of lie-ins, nightclub dance floors or drinking coffee while it
is still hot, you have to learn to be adaptable. Giving birth has not
made a totally new you, but you will need to acclimatise yourself
to a new child-friendly version of the adult you have created thus
far. This can be joyous (one good friend always hated late nights

and noisy bars, so she celebrated the excuses her baby gave her to avoid them) or miserable (a different friend was at her wit's end that she could no longer luxuriously read the *Sunday Times* in bed every weekend but had to grab articles on her phone in darkness, sitting beside a crib while settling her teething toddler), or just plain confusing. Motherhood is as big a culture shock as arriving in a foreign country where everything looks the same but you can't understand a word that's being said, the jet lag is killing you and your suitcase got lost en route, forcing you to stumble around in the same slightly grubby tracksuit your partner says makes you look like Kanye West, which is not a compliment. You're excited to be there, but you feel a bit discombobulated. Yes, that first year of motherhood is like jet lag with bad clothes.

The shock of a new little person's arrival hits as hard mentally as it does physically and socially, often more so. A 2016 report by NHS England revealed that up to one in five mothers experience problems such as postnatal depression and post-traumatic stress disorder. The 'baby blues' is not simply caused by hormones, but by many different factors including feeling unsupported by friends and family or doubting one's own ability to be a good mother, with chances of depression increasing if the mother has a history of mental health problems.

If ever you're going to negatively question your abilities as a human being, becoming a mother seems to be the time. And a mother's mental health problems not only affect the health of themselves but they can also have long-standing effects on children's emotional, social and cognitive development. With approximately 665,000 births a year in England, which means 66,500–133,000 women a year develop problems, there has never been a more crucial time for women to support each other, offer encouragement instead of judgement, and accept a new mother for the type of mother she wants to be instead of forcing an impossibly high standard on herself.

We assume that mothering a baby is the hardest part of the journey, but an essay by Vandita Morarka called 'Mothers and Mental Health' published in 2018 by The Health Collective highlights how mental-health issues don't automatically improve for the mother as the child grows up; in fact, the external pressure a woman feels around her role as a parent increases as the child gets older, as the set ideas of socio-cultural influencers increased, such as family, peers and the media about what a mother should look like and how she could do better for her child. At the start of her essay, Morarka shares a quote from Supreme Court Justice Ruth Bader Ginsburg. 'The pedestal you put women on is a cage,' she says, her words revealing how striving for *better* or *the best* comes at the cost of the personal health of the mother. Perfection is a terrible pressure.

Mama says: Cicely, 44

'When my firstborn arrived, I was scared to take my eyes off her – checking her tummy was going up and down breathing, and wheeling her with me into the toilet or shower so that I could watch her at all times. I loved every moment, but after a couple of weeks I was feeling stifled. I left her with my husband, saying I needed to pop out for half an hour. It was a hot and sunny day, I had the car windows open and turned the radio up to full volume and just wanted to feel free for 20 minutes without all the responsibilities of a tiny baby. That quick burst was all I needed. I drove home feeling liberated with a renewed sense of joy to be with my baby.'

Being yourself as a mother

Havovi Hyderabadwala, a clinical and forensic psychologist, speaks of 'supermom syndrome' and how this constant striving for idealism leaves women mentally and physically weakened and disabled in the long run. 'The mothers who live by "shoulds" and "musts" tend to burn out faster than the ones who allow themselves to make mistakes and acknowledge their limitations,' she argues. Of course, it's natural that mothers – especially first timers – are nervous about making mistakes, but the internal pressure we are under will take a toll, causing us to lose or gain weight, become sleep deprived, feel sad, and suffer with mood swings. Studies by Mental Health America, Postpartum Support International, and more, show how information from doctors and therapists, and a fair dose of wisdom and honesty from friends about the journey, will help mothers to find their feet with their new identity.

As mothers, we need to be kind to ourselves. You can recalibrate yourself by:

- Acknowledging the major life transition that you've gone through. Ask yourself questions: 'Who am I again?', 'Why do I feel so different?', 'How can I feel less anxious, tearful, tired?'
- Talking to people whom you trust and who can help you: your doctor, your midwife, your partner, the friends who care about you and understand the mothering experience, your NCT or antenatal group. Connect with people who are also first-time mothers. Sharing your thoughts will make you feel less isolated. Asking for help is not a show of weakness; it takes a village to raise a child, remember.
- Showing yourself compassion. Be a friend to yourself. Give yourself a break. If you haven't got dressed or washed today, who cares? What would you say to a mate who told you this? You'd say, 'Don't worry about that! You have so much going on! It's not important.' Talk to yourself kindly.
- Breaking up the day with small treats. A warm bath with relaxing lavender or uplifting sandalwood essential oils; a

five-minute neck massage from your partner or a sympathetic friend or colleague; a smoothie full of goodness and
your favourite flavours; half an hour with your Kindle and
a great book, or losing yourself with an audiobook.

- Getting outside for a walk around your neighbourhood or
  local park while you're pushing the pram. Fresh air and
  sunshine will boost your mood. Studies show that even
  moderate exercise is as effective at reducing mild depression as medication, while vitamin D will help you sleep
  soundly by resetting your circadian rhythm and boosting
  your 'happy hormone' serotonin levels.
- Turning on some music that makes you dance. Grab your
  baby, and wiggle around the room with abandon, singing
  and knowing that this too shall pass, this is natural, this
  is what most, if not all, women experience. Plus, dancing

(according to the *New England Journal of Medicine*) keeps your brain sharp while it is strengthening your stamina, bones and muscles.

- Not living vicariously through anyone else, whether celebrities, your friends on social media or your kids! Make your own news and events. Switching off comparisons will give you an instant boost.

Make self-care a habit

Even when your kids start to grow up and need you less desperately, self-care is still a must. Set dates in your diary that you will refuse to skip: a weekly yoga class, a bi-monthly date night, a once-a-month book club commitment. Pursue your interests – picking up old pre-kid ones or finding new ones – and write a journal, meditate, buy yourself flowers the first weekend of the month, keep scented candles next to the bath. The more you take care of yourself, the more you'll be able to take care of your children, whatever stage of this journey you're in.

Motherhood has been described as a process of living in constant fear, where you are forced to send your heart out into the world, outside the protective shell of your body, while you have to sit back and watch, helplessly. It can seem overwhelming. But going down rabbit holes of worry is as useful as making a cuppa in a chocolate teapot. I literally trained my brain to switch from a scary thought to something filled with gratitude or acceptance, or about what I was going to have for dinner. When I felt my mind hurtling towards a dark tunnel, I jumped off the train and landed in memories of my morning cuddles with my baby, or a funny episode from school. Flick that panic switch.

Mama says: Suzannah, 39

'When I had a newborn, I was told by a friend that mother-hood is the steepest learning curve I will ever experience, and that was precisely how I felt. This living, crying and unpredict-able baby girl came into my life and I was really out of sorts. A few weeks in, my husband said something to me that stung at the time, but he was absolutely right. He said, "I feel like you are sucking the fun out of this." Thankfully, that moment created a shift. I tried to rely on my own instincts rather than mimic my mum friends. The more authentic I felt, the more I could feel the joy. With so much access to information and opinions, I would encourage new parents to try to quiet the noise and hold clear intentions for what they want or need.'

Identity politics

Perhaps the most important book ever written about motherhood is Adrienne Rich's *Of Woman Born: Motherhood as Experience and Institution*. Written in 1976, a year after I was born, it still resonates deeply with women today, and it informed much of my doctoral studies on how evolving choices had changed motherhood in 20th-century Britain. Rich, a feminist poet and essayist, provoked questions about a mother's identity on every page, forcing me to challenge and confront stereotypes and notions that I had never considered before, and asking the reader to consider how external views of mothers damages the mother internally. She wrote,

> Unexamined assumptions that a "natural" mother is a person without further identity, one who can find her chief gratification in being all day with small children ... that maternal love is, and should be, quite literally

selfless. I was haunted by the stereotype of the mother whose love is "unconditional"; and by the visual and literary images of motherhood as a single-minded identity.

Rich explains how this drive from society to label a good mother as someone who has willingly let go of herself made her feel 'undeniable anger' and a 'tangle of irritations'. Her husband, her own mother and society expected her to give up her own identity and put her child firmly in front of any of her own needs or wants. But she couldn't do it. She was important, too. So are you.

We like to think we have evolved 40 years on: you can have it all; *girl power!* But have we really? The strict social conventions that women were scared to test in the 20th century have just been replaced with an undercurrent of whispering judgement and sniggering ridicule in the 21st. Women are still questioned and remarked on over everything, from how long they breastfeed to how their children behave in restaurants. The fathers rarely come up as a hot source of debate. The mother is still seen as the one who can make or break a child, and this unwritten requirement to become a servant to motherhood can promote feelings of unhappiness, hesitancy and guilt. 'I remember moments of peace when for some reason it was possible to go to the bathroom alone,' Rich notes. I remember that, too. Fifty years after Rich felt this, I had this same experience with my first baby: cherishing a couple of minutes that could still be mine, not handed over with everything else in my life to my offspring. Yes, tragically, a wee behind a closed door was held up as some sort of Shangri-La.

The parent trap

Today, mothers are shoved into stereotypes that can be easily dissected for the media, and other mothers, to understand, bait and judge. Are you a lawnmower mother (who cuts down any obstacles in your child's way, making them soft and spoilt), a tiger mum (who pushes her child to the point of overload), a free-range parent (who allows a child to raise itself like a feral animal), a helicopter parent (who hovers nervously overhead, teaching your child to be scared by its own shadow), or, even worse, are you a working mum (boo, hiss) who outsources her motherly responsibilities? Are you into 'attachment parenting', refusing to let your child leave your side 24/7? Are you authoritarian or permissive, uninvolved or too involved?

All these styles have fans and benefits, and all have critics and problems. None of this should bother you, however. What you need to concern yourself with is how to mix up your own blend of motherhood, by grabbing ingredients from these stereotypes that look tasty to you and then stirring them up into a satisfying concoction of your own. You don't have to serve it up to anyone else, or even write down the recipe. The most important thing is that you communicate clearly with your child what is going on in their world, with rules that are clear and the reasons for them explained, and you work on goals and expectations together, with a nurturing tone, allowing the child to have input when appropriate. Remember, your focus will have to shift with each child, as their temperament and abilities will differ, but a fair and balanced attitude set across the board, which shifts when needed, is a sound place to start.

You are still *you*

You've already had a lot of experiences in your life that are invaluable assets to take with you into motherhood: memories, experiences, jokes, explorations, ideas, qualifications and adventures, not to mention the friends you've accumulated by being you, and the level of acceptance you've settled into with your family because they've come to terms with you being you (and vice versa). It would be a shame to throw all this out with the used nappies – not just for yourself, but for your child. If you try to become something you're not, something will eventually explode. Authenticity is something we so often lack in our air-brushed, photoshopped and staged age, so cling on to your uniqueness with all your might. Tone it down a bit if you want to, take a few months off from your standard activities if you feel you would benefit from it, but never lose sight that having a child doesn't make you a *different person*. It's given you a new identity badge to wear that the world can see, pinned next to all the other identifiers that make you *you* (friend, daughter, sister, colleague, dancer, prancer, knitter, hiker, women's rights defender, and so on). Motherhood has just added another string to your beautiful bow, so you do *you* – everyone else is taken.

Be a personalised paragon of virtue

Virtues are habits of behaviour, heart and mind that we can turn into natural occurrences with practice, which in turn help to form our identity. As your child's protector, teacher and enabler, what do you want them to focus on alongside you? What do you want to focus on as you reconfigure your identity to fit your new role? Which do you and/or your child find easy or hard? Here are ten life skills worth nurturing to contemplate:

Courage	Humility
Fairness	Integrity
Fortitude	Loyalty
Gratitude	Positivity
Honesty	Wisdom

Mama says: Inger, 44

'My six-year-old son Harold and I were recently out in the garden, talking about motherhood, Mother Nature, and the different mothers found in the animal kingdom. After I had finished talking about nature versus nurture in child's language, he looked at me and said, "Mummy, you're like every kind of animal mixed up together." I laughed for a hundred reasons. It was funny because he made me sound like a wild, mangy, hysterical beast, and in that light, no truer words have ever been spoken, but also he'd picked up on the way in which mothers become courageous protectors, conscientious nurturers and brave fighters, free from manmade rules and stipulations when our gut instincts kick in. My son made me see that motherhood is a tie that binds us all, whether we have four legs or two.'

Is it all about timing?

Much of how you are perceived as a mother will depend on things outside your control. In a revealing 2007 essay in *Gender and Education* entitled 'Motherhood, choice and the British media: A time to reflect', the authors state that motherhood is still 'a contested area', and, despite the rapidly changing attitudes, traditions and laws encountered by British women since the 1950s, 'women's choices are open to scrutiny and judgement, deemed selfish or selfless' by the culturally persuasive media, particularly when considering the age at which they have a child.

Timing *is* important and something you need to think about thoughtfully and sensibly. You need to think about the impact motherhood will have on your career and your ability to continue with the same or similar professional life after you've had a child. You have to get your head around the changes to your lifestyle, to your finances, to your spare time, mental health and other relationships. People might tell you that you've had kids too early and you have not given your career time to take off, or they might tell you that you waited too long, thinking only about your work and not your long-term goals. But you must quieten these criticisms and follow your own clock, and choose a time that is right for you. If your career is important to you, own it. If it isn't, and you've always wanted to focus on building a family, own that too.

Mama says: Sophie, 40

'People often mention the pros and cons of being a working mum, but I simply don't see the cons anymore. I've quickly realised that I can control my life and how much I agree to travel and work. It's up to me to be unafraid to say no, to be efficient with my time and to find the right balance for me. I've also learned that my children get used to patterns and don't feel discomfort when I'm gone. The value I find in helping to support my family both emotionally and financially, as well as the pride and independence I feel being able to provide value both in the home and outside, means that I can bring that sense of pride and fulfilment to my children. I'm also a better employee since becoming a mother, taking what I have learnt from parenting to my team at work to become a better leader and decision maker.'

Make your choice about when, from your heart and your head, not from societal expectations or pressure. Bridget Jones, heroine of late 20th- and early 21st-century literature and film, frequently writes in her diary how she feels that her choices as a single, working woman are reduced to a series of judgements placed upon her by 'smug marrieds' and her mother, who taunts her with the 'tick-tock, tick-tock' of her biological clock. Bridget implies that even women of her generation have one main purpose, but even if they fulfil this purpose, as Bridget eventually does, they are judged for leaving it too late or for choosing the wrong man to build a family with, or for choosing the wrong birth plan.

Like Bridget, I was labelled a 'geriatric mother' when I was carrying William at 35 years old. It was an unflattering term that made me feel old and lazy, and every time I heard it it was a harsh reminder of the fertility worries that we'd had in order to get to this point, and the heartbreak that had halted our journey to parenthood until then. Older mothers are often placed in the category of being selfish, putting their careers first, and then indulging their child because of the overwhelming guilt that haunts them because of their dotage. Young mothers experience bias and negative identifiers, too, however, the media labelling them as work-shy or uneducated. When the media – especially in pages focused on women, sadly – enforce a notion that only mothers in their late twenties or early thirties are *good*, mothers need to band together. Make your own identity beyond something as meaningless as age.

Should I be enjoying motherhood more?

For many of us who desperately want to have children, the reality can be a little disappointing. The first few years are filled with long days full of often gruesome bodily fluids, temper tantrums (yours and theirs) and a feeling of never being able to catch up with your friends, your work or your sleep. You're a dopey dog trying to catch its tail. That's how you feel the world sees you, anyway. The motherhood you imagined – the matching outfits and sweet cuddles, the mutual adoration and magic moments – appear in glimmers, but they are the exception to the rule. In these moments of disappointment, I found it useful to reflect on the character-building nature of motherhood. If it had been an easy ride of hugs and cuteness, would I have felt tested? Would I have grown? Would I have built patience, kindness, resilience or bravery as tools that I can now claim to have in my back pocket? No. Motherhood is hard. We need to stop underplaying how we got to this point by pretending it is easy and be honest with ourselves and other mothers about the daily struggles, but we must also acknowledge the great skills and traits it has imbedded into our identity. Ask questions of your own mother and sister, confess your toughest times to friends, read articles or books by brave, truthful women you respect (Michelle Obama's autobiography is perfect for this). You'll get empowering feedback, I guarantee. Who knew you were such a multi-tasking, strong-stomached whirling dervish?

Dads have identity crises, too!

A pregnant wife, a new baby, a demanding toddler, a grumpy teen who towers over everyone else in the house: all these disruptors can leave your partner feeling raw and bewildered, too. We share some problems, and they have others to deal with. According to the Office of National Statistics, the number of British men taking on the role of stay-at-home parent has doubled over the last two decades and now stands at approximately 223,000, which can threaten their idea of traditional masculinity and their fear of failing to provide for their family. Also, sometimes men are confounded by their partner's lack of time and attention *for them* after she becomes a mother, which promotes resentment as they drop from the top place to lower down her list of priorities.

During both of my pregnancies, my husband Russ had an identity crisis and suffered what can only be described as a phantom pregnancy. He got cravings, gained weight, burst into tears for no obvious reason and even complained of sore nipples. There's a medical term for this, and it's increasingly common as modern men get more in touch with their feelings. 'Couvade syndrome is the clinical profession's term for a male experiencing a sympathetic or phantom pregnancy and comes from the French word *couver*, which means to brood or hatch,' my friend Dr Brian Beckham, a psychiatrist who specialises in relationship counselling, explained to me when I couldn't understand why my pregnancy would be so hard for Russ to handle. 'The expectant father may feel his masculinity is being diminished, while his partner will often feel like he is attempting to take the attention and care away from her.'

Russ certainly tried! Four weeks before I was due to give birth to our first child we had to rush to hospital in the middle of the night. 'There's a lot of pain,' the soon-to-be daddy explained to a nurse. 'On a scale of one to ten, how much pain are you in?' We'd been told in our pre-natal classes that I would be asked this repeatedly as labour progressed to work out if and when I would need an epidural. Russ had been adamant that giving birth would only score about a five and that I probably wouldn't need drugs, just a positive attitude and a bit of deep-relaxation breathing. 'About a nine,' my well-built, six-foot-three-inch husband winced. 'It's really bad.' The nurse lifted up his injured foot and shook her head while looking at my bulging belly. 'You would not believe the number of men we see in casualty with silly injuries like this when their wives are pregnant. It's as if they want attention.'

I was angry. Wasn't this journey *really* all about the mother? 'I believe it is a real condition that reveals the mental and physical anxiety that an estimated 10 to 20 per cent of men experience when their partner is expecting,' said Dr Beckham. 'Some medical studies have suggested that any male partner co-habiting with a pregnant woman will experience hormonal shifts in his testosterone levels, starting at 12 weeks through several weeks postpartum, which are meant to help create a stronger father–child bond.'

How to help him handle his new identity

This type of fatherly identity crisis represents a psychological and physiological desire to share in this special time, from pregnancy to having a three-month-old, but what about after that? How can a man adapt to his new role in a way that is healthy for you both? And how can you help? Get him involved – having Dad take on responsibilities will give you a break, and the more time he spends alone with your child, the more capable and confident you'll *both* feel when he's in charge. Encourage him to play, praise, teach, hug, borrow bits from his own childhood and his relationship with his own dad that worked. The best thing that you, as a mother, can do to help your partner through an identity crisis – or panic, perhaps we should call it – is to remind him that all that your child really wants is his time and attention. They want to hang out. Encourage him to get into a football team together, introduce his child to his favourite music, get his old Lego out of his parents' loft and build stuff. Much like mothers, a lot of fathers' identity crises come from wondering if they are *good enough*. He is. You are. You both are.

Becoming a team

If you've been Miss Independent your whole life, suddenly moving around your world like a travelling circus will come as a bit of a shock. My life was made immeasurably smoother and cooler when I become adept at asking my partner, family and friends for help. At the start, I thought I had to do everything – so my husband let me. After a while of me quietly seething with resentment, we had a conversation. 'I don't know what you need me to do,' he said, and I knew in that instant it was true.

Fatherhood was as foreign to him as motherhood was to me, and I did have a tendency to tell him that he was doing things wrong if he did try to take charge. I scared him away, and the magnitude of the role of father scared him away ... and I felt alone. We worked hard to become a team and these tips worked for us:

If one of you is a natural leader, and the other doesn't resent it, one of you can set the agenda, the schedule and the division of childcare. Keep to the plan, unless it really has to be altered. I now tell my husband which kids' party he will be attending at weekends, where he has to be, what he has to take, and which parents he'll know there. It cuts out our old system where we both thought we had to go and be trapped in a trampoline park, or both of us would try to get out of going. Kids' parties at weekends are now his accepted *thing*.

We support each other in front of the children, raising disagreements in calmer, quieter moments away from their ears. This stops the children from getting confused, and it means that we can discuss things away from the pressure of the moment.

We look for, and encourage, each other's key interests I am a very neat person; my husband is very clean, so I make sure the house is free from clutter and disruption on a daily basis, and he'll give the bath a weekly clean. Turn chores into meditative practice. I actually enjoy the instant reward of vacuuming, so I have taken over that part of the housework routine. My husband enjoys the physical workout and fresh air he gets from cleaning our car, so he does that. I look after the children's admin; he looks after the adults' admin, just giving each other the highlights rather than a full download.

We noticed that working as a team made us less stressed It even made us more romantically inclined towards the other. When you're tired and your partner puts the laundry on ... well, that's alluring.

Becoming a team has made us better communicators To get the boring stuff of life done quicker, we've had to learn to listen better, talk clearer, problem solve and manage conflict. This not only helps us to stay on top of paying the bills but also in all aspects of our marriage.

When we work smoothly as a team, we are aware that we're inspiring our kids to do the same, which pushes us even more.

Friends who have gone through divorce have told me that teamwork is still a part of their unmarried life – perhaps even more so. They work hard to back up their partner in front of the children, they never talk badly about their partner behind their back, and they try to be cooperative with scheduling. They have taken a businesslike approach to parenting that keeps them punctual, polite and respectful, which their children then mimic. This, they say, has helped make the difficult transition easier for everyone.

Teamwork is about diplomacy and fairness, not about being a dog's body. Keep each other in check and call out on imbalance when you feel it.

Ten empowering tracks

Music to help you embrace the power of your new mama identity.

'Fight Song' by Rachel Platten

'Glad You Came' by The Wanted

'The Sweetest Devotion' by Adele

'Put Your Records On' by Corinne Bailey Rae

'You Came' by Kim Wilde

'Treasure' by Bruno Mars

'Stronger' by Kelly Clarkson

'What I Never Knew I Always Wanted' by Carrie Underwood

'Hold On' by Wilson Phillips

'I Hope You Dance' by Lee Ann Womack

Mama says: Abby, 41

'I found the journey to becoming a mother very confusing to start with. There was no doubt that I was ready but I totally lost a sense of who I was. We were the first of our friends to have kids, and I felt totally confused with no support network. My husband went back to work and my old media friends were off being busy and fabulous, and I felt terribly alone. I adored being with my children, but I still felt as if the essence of me had been eaten up by the whole process. It was an extraordinary time, like a rebirth really. Now my kids are older I am finding more time for myself, my career and my hobbies. I am finding myself again and I really like what I'm finding. I am finding more joy than ever in being outdoors, in cold-water wild swimming, making friends with people who have the same hobbies as me, being creative and taking on the world.'

Your PG rating

Think about each of the aims listed below and write your thoughts in a notebook. Reread them and remind yourself of these aims as you go through life as a mother, putting them into practice whenever you can. Remember that the intention is not to put yourself in a position of feeling that you must be a perfect mother but someone who is learning, sharing and growing with her children and family.

The Ps:

Purpose Think about what kind of mother you want to be.

Perspective You are now a mother, but you are still *you* – how can you combine the two?

Presence You will adapt as your child grows, your identity is fluid, you can handle change.

The Gs:

Gratitude Be thankful for the solid groundwork of virtues you built before you became a parent.

Goals Find positive ways to teach your children to be confident in their own identity.

Going for it It's never too early to start guiding your children towards values that are important to you and your family. Think about the values that you want to ensure your children understand at a young age and how to make them values that they can practise in their young lives, i.e. teaching them how to share with their friends, reminding them how to say sorry, daring them to try a new food.

TAKE A DEEP BREATH, MAMA

Let go of the pressure you feel to be a certain person or a certain type of mother, or to restrict yourself to an identity that is neither the old you or the new you. The beauty of the human condition is that it changes, rebuilds, fortifies and washes away. Feelings, emotions, perceptions and physical responses to pain and pleasure can all adapt; they can all be manipulated. Hold dear the things you cherish, wave goodbye to the things you don't. Pay less attention to the outside (external pressure, external judgements, external expectations, external appearance) and pay more attention to how you feel inside. This is your truth. This is what your child needs. This is what you need.

2

Give Up the Guilt

'Guilt to motherhood is like grapes to wine'

Fay Weldon

I've never done well with guilt. As a child I was one of those timid creatures who'd rather stay cowering silently, red-faced, behind the grey-school-uniformed shoulders of louder, more confident youngsters than risk making an exhibition of myself and feeling bad about it for weeks. I have always been very serious. 'Your soul has been here before,' some soothsaying octogenarian who smelled of gingernuts and dust announced when I was a teen, glumly stumbling around Camden Market in my Dr Martin boots. This sounded rather mystical and exciting until she added, 'So your life is going to be weighed down with insurmountable feelings of guilt.'

Depending on my hormones or alcohol levels, anything has the ability to make me feel bad: if I eat too much, exercise too little, gossip too much, or listen too little ... In paranoid moments, I still feel bad about telling a dear friend that her husband looks like one of the barrow boys from *EastEnders* (I thought it was a compliment; she didn't) and turning into a bit of a Bridezilla and banning children from my wedding (to the distress of the women, with whom I now belong, who feel guilty if they leave their offspring overnight), and I get wincing flashbacks to the time I put my kid brother on a skateboard and attached him to the back of a milk float and, of course, he fell off. You can imagine, then, how I got sucked down the rabbit hole of motherhood guilt. I was going pretty crazy for a while. I was Miss Guilty of Guiltsville, Guiltenstein.

Proudly human, not a machine

It has been said that you can't please all the people all the time, but everyone seems to expect perfection from mothers. Do they think we get impregnated and then magically become Virgin Mary types, acquiring halos, the patience of a saint and an inability to complain about even the most difficult of circumstances (riding a donkey in the final trimester, giving up booze while breastfeeding, trying to hold a conversation with a miniature beast hanging from your thigh)? Well, sod that. It's hard enough trying to be perfect when you have free time. When you're parenting, you have to settle for acceptable. And that goes for your appearance, your house, your ability to communicate – everything.

'Those who mind don't matter, and those who matter don't mind'

If I had a dollar for every time I saw that saying plastered on a mug or posted on Facebook I'd be living on South Beach drinking a mojito while my children were being entertained by a Mary

Poppins simulacrum in immaculately pressed linens right now. Mummies need to work extra hard to remember this clever quip. Buy that tacky mug and drink from it every day. Because as soon as you announced your pregnancy, I bet you were inundated with well-meaning, over-bearing know-it-alls offering advice and suggestions about how to raise your child and regaling you with the horrors that would prevail if you rebel from *their* prescribed way. Suddenly, so much is expected from you – and not just from your boss or your mother-in-law, but also from society. Choose who you will allow to influence you, because the more people you choose, the guiltier you'll feel when things go awry. And they *will* go awry.

Think forward

If you're reading this book while pregnant, rush off to a café or supermarket right now and observe the parents you see trying to control their porridge-splattered, octopus-limbed offspring in public. Regard the look of guilt that passes across their furrowed brow and bloodshot eyes every time they catch someone throwing a sideways glance. Once your child arrives, you join the side of the harassed and tired, and you'll realise what a complete twerp you were for judging a parent when you knew nothing about it. And never gossip about your friends who have unruly, obnoxious teens, muttering under your breath that your little cherubs could never grow so wild. They might. Check your judgement at the door. Motherhood should make you kinder and more forgiving.

A side of guilt to go, please

Nothing makes mountains out of molehills like motherhood. I remember being pregnant and planning a drug-free, doula-led natural birth. When I had to have an emergency C-section, I felt terrible guilt because earthy-crunchy types had told me it was impossible to bond unless your child wriggled its way out of your peekachoo. During William and my second night together, I allowed the nurses to watch him for a few hours so that I could get to sleep. I felt terrible guilt about this because it proved that I wasn't coping already, didn't it? At three weeks, after enduring the hell of mastitis, my mother insisted that I let her feed a bottle to my baby, instead of letting him try to suckle my inflamed boobs. My chest felt like two bags of rocks and razors but I still felt guilty that I wasn't able to do easily what is supposed to come naturally – the boob brigade had told me he'd refuse my melons forever if I offered him a bottle too early.

I had a list of shame I carried around like a festering nappy bag during my first year of motherhood, and it tarnished the experience for me. How many of these do you share?

- Drinking two margaritas on my first girls' night out when he was only six weeks old.
- Giving him a name that is very boring/classic instead of something wild like Ryder or Hudson.
- Letting him roll off the bed while I was checking my email.
- Thinking that it would be more fun to dress him if he was a girl.
- Telling a friend that I thought that, in a certain light, he looked like Yoda from Star Wars.
- Wishing he would just shut the #%&* up... frequently.
- Tapping away on my laptop while he picked dried Cheerios of the carpet next to my desk.
- Feeding him his favourite foods (yoghurt, hummus, cheese) instead of pushing vegetables.

- Allowing him to crawl around on the dirty floor of various establishments.
- Giving him a taste for ice cream at 11 months.
- Adoring him theatrically to the point of smothering.
- Allowing him to foster an unhealthy addiction to Peppa Pig.
- Working when other mothers were spending all their time singing to their kids.
- Turning a blind eye when he chewed his friends' toys.
- Not rushing him to the doctor's when he had a cough, thinking he would 'toughen it out' (which he did) and forgetting to turn on his humidifier on a number of occasions.
- Moaning to my husband when he got in from work, because although I loved my son, I loved him more when he was (a) asleep; (b) cuddling me quietly; or (c) exploding with glee. The hours of whining, grizzling and screaming were hard to love.

Leave the guilt behind

Around the time of William's first birthday I realised that I was fed up with guilt jostling alongside me on my already tiring journey, and I decided to kick it to the kerb. None of the horror stories I'd heard or the fears I had had came to fruition. Or they had, but they weren't as bad as I had imagined, and I found I had this mama superpower that allowed me to just *know* stuff that would make his life better. Despite my 12-month-long walk of shame, William and I have an incredible bond, and I've decided to forgive myself for the less-than-show-home things I did in my first year of motherhood. There really is no blueprint for perfection. Being a mother is so important and so challenging that we have to give ourselves credit rather than criticism. Save the guilt for when it's justified, like the time I didn't bother to read a sign at Universal Studios and took a three-year-old William on an innocent bus ride – past Jaws and King Kong – and he screamed for ten minutes while Japanese tourists took photos of him. I have sleepless nights about the untold damage that did him. Will the boy ever be brave enough to swim in The Hamptons or eat bananas?

Tit-topia

Discussions around breastfeeding eat new mothers alive more than anything else. We are all told that breast is best for its health benefits for you and your child, and for your wallet and the environment, but it is the most personal of decisions for you to make. After attempts at both methods to get my husband involved, I found nursing easier, which some people couldn't understand. Instead of having to clean bottles, measure formula and warm milk (often in the dark) I could just whip out my 'modesty cloak', as I jokingly called my nursing cloak, point and aim, but not all women can do this, and they shouldn't feel forced to. If you fear that you aren't producing enough milk, or that you're in a lot of pain, or you find the whole process mortifyingly embarrassing, don't do it. If you know that you've given it your best shot but it's not working, you should be able to move on to the bottle without beating yourself up. Give it a go – it really can be magical, and I still miss it – but stop when it stops being good for your mental health. And remember, it simply isn't true that by not giving your child breast milk you are ruining him or her forever. The truth is that it *does* help, but it's not as if you can look around a room of teenagers and spot the boob-fed one, or that Oxbridge has a disproportionately high number of breast-sucklers. The best thing for a baby is a confident, content mother.

Mama says: Lorna, 31

'The worst guilt I have experienced so far in my entire life was when I started introducing formula at six months and stopped breastfeeding shortly afterwards. Withdrawing all that natural goodness from my beautiful baby and giving her a processed substitute made me feel guilty, but the real shame I felt was because I was secretly so relieved that the experience of nursing, which I had never enjoyed, was over.'

People pleaser? Not me

In the first years of motherhood, I would too often find myself in a baby or toddler class surrounded by women who insisted that little Jonny was not allowed to watch television or eat sugar or wee in the bath. As they sermonised, I'd try to hide the fruit pouch that William was holding, or sneak Matilda away from the screen I'd bribed her with so that I could chat to a friend and nod in agreement. I felt it wasn't worth the hassle of being controversial, so I sat small, with my guilt and fear of reproach shushing me.

Fast forward a couple of years, post feeling the guilt. I was rushing my kids to school, clutching some shop-bought cupcakes for the teacher-appreciation lunch. 'Ooh, the other mums are going to judge you for those!' the headmistress laughed as we passed each other in the corridor. 'We've had a parade of home-made bakes coming in this morning.' I stopped, held my cupcakes aloft, and growled, 'Let them try!' in the manner of *Braveheart*. I was working for a city newspaper, trying to write my PhD dissertation, and participate in my kids' school community. I didn't even have the time to take the cakes out of the wrapping and pretend I'd made them (which is something many other mothers do, and good luck to them!).

I'd learnt during the first few years finding my feet as a mama that the only people I need approval from are my children and myself, and that I do not need to give or withhold my approval from anyone else either. How dare I? We all have our own hurdles to jump. I needed to be my own advocate and cheerleader, and so do you. If my children ate shop-bought fruit and veg pouches because I was too busy to buy, scrub, peel, cook, blend and store homemade organic meals, which they tended to hurl against the wall or make finger paints with anyway, or if I rushed to the supermarket to buy cakes so that I could finish an essay by the deadline, so be it. You want to judge me? Bring. It. On.

Listen to your heart

If you're still feeling guilty, try to work out why. Are you bombarded with an external cacophony of judgements and opinions? As a mother, you really want to shift to the internal. Listen to your heart, not the external mutterings of people who don't know your story, your current situation, your child's temperament. Think about how you want to mother, not how anyone else wants you to mother.

You can understand and explain some motherhood guilt and self-doubt by acknowledging that you are suffering from Imposter Syndrome, that internal fear that we're not good enough and that people are going to find us out at any minute. I had it when I was made the editor-in-chief of a magazine at 29 years old and assumed it had been a terrible mistake, even when the magazine became a success. Often, as mothers, it seems easier to ignore the successes we have, or joyful moments of connection, and focus on the parts of our day that reconfirm how rubbish we feel. We remember the one minute of nagging before school instead of the 20 minutes of snuggling and reading *Charlotte's Web*. We remember how all the other mothers seemed so calm and organised while we look like a wreck. We remember our panic as we couldn't control their two-minute tantrum instead of the fun they had on their two-hour play date, which we'd gone out of our way to organise. Reset your Imposter Syndrome by reminding yourself you are this child's parent, you are good enough, and by regarding your ridiculously high standards for what they are and giving yourself a break. Find one or two confidants you trust and ask them if they ever feel the same (they will), and write a list of positive comments that you've received from your children, partner, friends or strangers, and reread the list when you're feeling sunk. It's a pretty good list, right? You are not an imposter, you deserve to be in this role.

Think about the bigger picture

Motherhood amplifies, highlights and exaggerates situations and feelings: sometimes minute occurrences can take on a life of their own until you believe that the world is ending. My suggestion is that you step back from the specific and take a global view. Will the world really end if you forgot the nappy bag and little bunny has to travel home from Grandma's with a dirty nappy? No. Will your child fall if he tries to climb that tree? Maybe. Will you have to deal with a tired and ratty child if you travel as a family to a new, exciting place? Probably. But, does the positive outweigh the negative? *Yes.* Don't sweat the small stuff. Look at the bigger picture. You will drive yourself nutty if you worry over every tiny little thing.

Mama says: Jayne, 37

'The guilt never goes away 100 per cent. It is still a very familiar emotion to me. It was my decision to break up the family unit when my children were five and seven, and introduce them to a childhood of ferrying themselves and their belongings between two homes twice a week. I feel guilt when I see them having to remember to carry to school not just what they need that day but also what's needed for the next three days, and I feel guilt when their father's girlfriend has spent the day baking cakes with them and I haven't. And that's just the beginning. I manage my guilt by believing that the more influences they are exposed to, the more rounded they will become.'

Did I really do this to my own mother?

Becoming a mother changes your relationship with your own mother. Regardless of whether she did everything right or most things wrong, you will now understand her better. You'll realise how tough it was for her, especially before the days of easily accessible childcare and online supermarket shopping. You might feel bad today about your teenage strops and swearing outbursts. I now feel terrible that I took up most of the space in my adolescent diary saying how mean my mum was because – as I can now appreciate – she was trying to instil some pretty good values and traits in me. But your mum doesn't resent you, so don't start to feel guilty about that too. As you're finding out yourself, it is a mother's lot to take occasional abuse, because you are your child's safe space. You are the one they can trust to keep loving them when they become unlovable.

Be your own best friend

Embrace the guilt, shrug it off and adopt your 'this is me, like it or lump it' attitude as your new best friend. Your occasionally thoughtless partner, smug school mums who make it look effortless, your single, contraception-quaffing pals who look at you with distaste when you discuss tummy bugs ... they can all just get on with it and you can shake it off and soak in your achievements, small or large. Feeling guilty about something you (a) can't change; or (b) don't need to is as beneficial to you as a bicycle is to a fish. Let go:

- Watch *Mommie Dearest* – see, you're not that bad!

- Read any Dickens novel – you look even better now.
- Crack open a box of macaroons with other new mums and let them talk.
- Acknowledge that 'this too shall pass', because everything does.
- Breathe deeply and swig Bach's Rescue Remedy.
- Tell your partner how important it is that he or she confirms/affirms what a good mother you are on a daily basis.
- Talk with a life coach about the feelings of inferiority or insecurity you have.
- Think positively. As long as your child is loved and cared for, you're doing great. Who cares if he ate mud in the park today?

Mama says: Susie, 38

'Some mums find it hard doing household chores or working from home, as they think they should be entertaining their children constantly, but I believe that it's a good balance for children to be aware and to see that cleaning, gardening, sitting at a desk typing, etc., is all part of everyday life and needs to be done. I think that my girls have a full, fun and varied life with gym, ballet, swimming and play dates, but it is just as important for them to entertain themselves at home playing with their toys or make-believe games while I get on, or I eat my lunch in peace – and I refuse to feel guilty about it. Freya now loves to help and has her own duster and vacuum. Alice still prefers to play with mud rather than actually help, but at least she can play in the mud on her own!'

Don't feel guilty about telling them off

Sometimes our children are not sweet: they are terrors – and if you ever had to pull them up on something, they probably deserved it. It is not your job to raise kids who will grow up to be rock stars or rocket scientists; if they want that badly enough, they will find a way, with your support, but it is your job to raise kids who are polite and kind. Having a good grip on etiquette will make their lives easier, even in the workplace a long way down the line, and a focus on courtesy and thoughtfulness can never start too soon. Some kids react to a softly, softly approach, whereas others respond to a stern word. My son sets himself straight after we have a matter-of-fact chat about how he could be better; my daughter needs more of a 'we'll get through this mistake together' hug. No child responds to, or bene-fits or improves from, physical discipline. A smack on the bottom says more about your inability to control your frustration than your desire to raise a kind child. All corporal punishment will do is teach your child to lash out in anger, to control people younger or smaller than themselves using violence, and that aggression is what adults are allowed to do. If they're driving you insane, walk away, if you can, until you can reclaim your composure (I infrequently tell my husband to take over and then I leave the house or plug in some music and leave them to it), or if you can't, take a deep breath, punch a pillow, scream in the garden, but know that attacking them will just make you feel worse, make them feel worse and set a bad prece-dent. If their behaviour is unacceptable (and I'm talking about being deliberately unacceptable, not a 13-month-old throwing food on the floor as he experiments with spoons, or a child refusing to wear appropriate shoes), they need to be told so. Don't let them get away with murder, but find a method that works for you and your child without losing your composure, your voice or your self-restraint. I say all this knowing that it is hard and that you need nerves of steel to raise children, and that sometimes you won't like them very much and you'll mutter a barrage of swear words under your breath just to get through that episode – and that's okay.

The confession box

Where can we go to get support about the moments that, as new mothers, we are not proud of? If your partner does not understand you, talk to friends, women who have been there before who will not judge you. These people don't have to be mothers; they can just be people who have been through moments of doubt and negativity but who managed to turn it around into certainty and positivity. Don't beat yourself up. If you are finding it impossible to move on, talk to your health visitor or doctor, or even consider hiring a life coach or going for parenting therapy. It might sound dramatic, but sometimes it helps for someone outside your inner circle to ask you questions without judgement or agenda. Outside help can clarify the situation while acting as an unbiased sounding board.

Misery loves company

Try to avoid the trap that many mothers fall into: surrounding themselves with other exhausted, frazzled new mothers who do nothing but moan, groan and act as if their world has come to an end while boring everyone with countless photos of little Jimmy in dungarees, little Jimmy in a swing, little Jimmy asleep. I was certainly guilty of this during William's first year on planet Earth. I'd get together with a lovely bunch of interesting women, and we'd moan about our lazy husbands, whine about our lack of sleep and gripe about never getting to drink our coffee while it was hot. Then, we'd discuss at great length incredibly dull things like pooing, dribbling and crawling. Blimey – these were amazing women, and motherhood had turned them (and me!) into hideous, old hags. Then, one wise friend broke free and declared war on our motherhood misery. 'Instead of sitting around in coffee shops grumbling,' she proclaimed, 'we will get our partners to babysit and one evening a month we can go to the cinema, then dinner, and not discuss our family life.' We felt cultured, in touch and energised. We talked about stuff beyond our children. We always included a few non-mothers too, who told us off if we went down a miserable path. Confess, share, download and offload the problems, issues and dilemmas, then look for solutions and soul-soothers. Do not dwell on the dark side.

It's a hard-knock life

The hardest thing for me to let go of is the idea that I can't protect William and Matilda all the time. I would wrap them in bubble wrap and keep them in a padded room if I thought I could. The first time your baby hurts herself you will feel terrible. You'll probably weep and wail more than she will. But you can't be their protection officer 24/7. They will crawl, climb, walk and mix with other kids who have a penchant for pinching. You just have to make their environment as safe as possible for them to expand and learn in, and be there for them if something does go a bit wrong. When he was 14 months old, William decided that it would be fun to bounce on the sofa. I was sitting next to him and thought it looked fun too. Then three seconds later, while I was still sitting next to him, one vigorous bounce threw him onto a table – and straight into hospital for three stitches. As I pinned him down under the bright lights so that the surgeon could work, William wailed and I wailed. Why did I let him bounce? What had I done to my precious child? The truth is that I was next to him and nothing could have been done. Fast forward five years, I've flown to a different city 1,000 miles away to defend my doctoral dissertation (a gruelling, intimidating procedure where three or four academics question a student on their thesis). I walk out a doctor and call my husband, who tells me that in the 24 hours I've been gone four-year-old Matilda has fallen off a wall and broken her arm. I should have been there! I ran off, thinking only about my own dreams, and my little girl is in agony! Or not – she could have done it anywhere, at any time. This was not my fault. All kids will get knocks, grazes and a bash around the earhole from a bigger kid with a sharing phobia. When guilt kicks in (a) remember what doesn't kill us makes us stronger; and (b) ask your own mother for a recap of your childhood injuries which you don't remember (aged three, I apparently ironed my own thigh to get the wrinkles out after a long bath, and yet I have no memory of this).

Mama mantras to help you forget mistakes

- First, do a bit of honest self-analysis. What do you feel guilty about? Pinpoint the cause. Should you feel guilty about certain things? Are you letting things slide? If so, change.
- Make a list of top priorities for you, your child and your family as a working unit. Prioritise what matters to *you*, not other families – we're all different. Then stick to that list, and let the small stuff that's not high up on it look after itself.
- Oscar Wilde said, 'One should always be a little improbable.' Take your new-found mummy-in-state-of-constant-madness

as something delightfully improbable, rather than something you should feel guilty about.

- I hate to sound like a Barry White record but, mama, all you are guilty of is loving too much and trying to maintain a little bit of your old self. If you didn't care how your child would react to you working/having a smidgen of a social life, you wouldn't worry. Understand that the guilt is a sign of your devotion.

- Learn to say no to things that in the past you would have just agreed to. As a mother, you now don't have the time to just go along with everything for an easy life. Don't over-book. Don't rush around trying to get to every birthday party, family party or work do. You can become a social butterfly again when the kids flit off to college. Until then, enjoy having a legitimate excuse to stay home and watch *Strictly Come Dancing*.

- 'The thing that is really hard, and really amazing, is giving up on being perfect and beginning the world of becoming yourself.' When journalist Anna Quindlen gave that advice, I bet she had mothers in mind. Who said we had to be perfect? Let's face it, our kids will blame us for everything anyway, so let's let go of this anxious fear that we are not doing good enough. Just by reading this book, it shows that you take being a mother very seriously and think about it even in the limited time you have away from your nipper. Just keep doing your best.

- Children are smarter than we think. Before they can hold proper conversations, they're learning how to manipulate us. Don't feel bad about saying no. It is your job to keep them healthy and safe, so stick to your principles – even if they give you a dirty look or throw themselves down onto the floor in anger. They will get over it, so you have to get over it, too.

- Live in the moment. Don't worry about what is in the past. Learn your lessons and move on. The only benefit to feelings of guilt is that it allows you look at your emotions, address problem areas and change. Do that. Then move on. Guilt is self-absorbing and self-defeating, and, sadly, you just don't have the time for navel-gazing any more, mamas.

Your PG rating

Think about each of the aims listed below and write your thoughts in a notebook. Reread them and remind yourself of these aims as you go through life as a mother, putting them into practice whenever you can. Remember that the intention is not to put yourself in a position of feeling that you must be a perfect mother but as someone who is learning, sharing and growing with her children and family.

The Ps:

Purpose Your aim is to raise happy, healthy kids, not to fit into a societal stereotype. Are you living that?

Perspective We're all just trying our best, balancing a million things. Should we be kinder to ourselves, and other women around us who are climbing obstacles we know nothing about? Yes!

Presence Forget what you've done; don't worry about the future. What can you do today to feel content?

The Gs:

Gratitude Be thankful for your child's resilience and love; be thankful for your self-awareness and self-compassion.

Goals Build relationships with people who support you; step away from those who make you feel bad about yourself.

▶

Going for it Hold your truth. It is not possible to love every minute of motherhood. It is at times boring, tiring and frustrating. Accept your emotions without feeling guilty and correct your default setting as you go forward. Repeat after me: I'm doing my best. I am the best mama for my child.

TAKE A DEEP BREATH, MAMA

If you feel internal guilt – from your heart, your gut, or your head – look at yourself as an outsider would. Observe with fresh eyes how you love your children, make their life easier and sweeter, balance your commitments, support your community, and then plan ahead. But appreciate that any attempt at perfection will go awry, unnoticed or fail, because you are a mother, not a Stepford Wife. Your children love your foibles and faux pas as much as they love your fawning and fabulosity. You're *their* mama. They may envy a friend's Nerf gun or sparkly slippers, but when your child is old enough, ask them what they think about you. They wouldn't swap you for the world.

3

Choose Freedom

'Once you sign on to be a mother, that's the only shift they offer'

Jodi Picoult, My Sister's Keeper

One Saturday in December, I was lucky enough to head into the countryside for a yoga and meditation retreat. I'd been feeling a bit like Freddie Mercury in the 'I Want to Break Free' video and needed time away from work–mama mode, when I felt I'd either been trapped at my desk or attached to the washing machine. It was a freezing, blue-sky December day full of delicious food, deep stretching and good women, but everyone was feeling a bit guilty that they were there, treating themselves to something nice, rather than running themselves ragged planning the perfect Christmas for everyone else. 'It's such a stressful time, there's so much to do,' one mother of three said to the instructor. 'People have such high expectations of what I need to do! Most of all, I have such high expectations of what I need to do!'

Sensing many of the group might have been bound by these physical and mental restraints, the instructor – a wise woman who wielded an air of calm like a magic wand – stopped this anxious woman mid-rant: 'You need to be free of these expectations. You know everyone is concerned with themselves, not looking at you? You know your family would rather have you happy than have a perfectly set table on Christmas Day?'

'I know that, deep down, but I feel a weight on me to find perfect gifts, be the perfect host ...'

'Shake off that weight!' she said. 'You deserve to escape for a day. You run around after your kids, you run around after your boss. You have earned a mental and physical break. Choose freedom from your day-to-day life to allow yourself to bring fresh air and new ideas into it. Even if it's just for a few hours!'

She then taught us about a condition called 'the comparative mind' which clings to us, especially women, restricting them from living their fullest, happiest life, always second guessing and looking over our shoulder for someone to tell us we're doing it wrong compared with everyone else. It really upset me to hear these women share their stories of comparison, paranoia and guilt – these strong, kind, generous women – and I stewed on it for weeks afterwards, working out when and how I'd become settled enough to switch off my own comparative mind and how I could distil it to share with others.

Leave behind your comparative mind

Do you mother through a lens of what your mother did? Or your husband's ex-wife? Your best friend or worst enemy? Are you running your family life not from instinct, or genuine wants or needs that would make you all content, but from a position of constant comparison to others, or comparison to a fantasy that you're holding for some reason? Keeping up with the Joneses is what we used to call it – and even if the Joneses in your scenario is your vision of your perfect self, it's exhausting and fruitless, and it doesn't make you any better. Why?

No one is perfect You are comparing yourself to a myth. Even your memories aren't foolproof. You might look back on family Christmases as wonderful and worry that you won't give your kids the same joy, but you've probably glossed over the drunken uncle, the dry turkey and the constant squabbling, as you rushed from one event to another. And we must get better at remembering this in our age of social media. We are seeing a perfectly crafted snapshot of a moment, not the whole truth.

We all have different advantages, and disadvantages, because life isn't fair. Comparing ourselves to others is fruitless because some people will always have more than us, which makes us resentful, and some will always have less, which makes us feel guilty.

Your children will see your behaviour, and mimic it They will start to question their own abilities compared to their school friends, or the size of their house compared to the neighbours. They will learn to resent the successes of others, rather than celebrating them – turning allies into rivals. You – and they – need to adopt an attitude of support. Circumstances fluctuate: we all have good and bad times. I have re-set my mindset so that when a friend tells me news that I would once feel envious of, I rejoice in it, thankful that there are still opportunities out there, and use it as motivation to achieve my goals. We all rise together.

By choosing to compare yourself to others only as a means of self-improvement rather than one-upmanship, you are freeing yourself from the emotional guilt that comes when you feel a creeping jealousy towards the people around you. Freeing yourself from a comparative mindset will allow you to focus on what you are doing, and how you are doing it.

Comparing ourselves to others – or an unattainable image of ourselves – is all a waste of time anyway. Buddhism tells us that fundamentally all humans have to go through the same four phases of life, regardless of money, power or beauty. We are born, we age, we get ill and we die – all of us, no matter how well our son does in his school exams or how quickly we lose our baby weight. What matters, teaches the Buddha, and what makes our existence worthwhile, is self-acceptance, meaningful relationships and a clear purpose. We can only get this from within. It doesn't matter what the woman next door has parked on her driveway.

You can't pour tea from an empty pot

My wise friend Marginy, a public health professor and mother of two young boys, has always emphasised to me the value of self-care, especially for mothers. She told me to stop thinking that making time for myself meant that I was being lazy or weak, or that other mothers might give side-eye and gossip about me being self-indulgent. She pointed out that mothers are often the *teapot* of the family: the instrument from which everyone else gets quenched, warmed, nourished and comforted. If the teapot is empty, there's nothing to give and everyone goes without.

The pursuit of liberty and the need to work

To many of us, a true freedom from motherly constraints comes from working. We love our children, and they are our priority, but to escape into our jobs and use our brains differently feels like a blast of fresh air. If your child is cared for appropriately, you should never feel guilty about deciding to pursue your own career and goals, and enjoying time away from the domestic grind. When the work–life balance is somewhat even, women often find themselves enjoying the quality time they now feel mentally able to give to their children, over the bigger quantity of time staying at home and being with them all day would give. Do what is right for you, and what can be made to work for your family, then embrace the differences between the two worlds. And enjoy the commute, if you can: those minutes when you belong to no one and can listen to what you want, daydream, catch up with friends, beholden only to your (hopefully efficient) local transport system! Try not to think about what awaits you in the office, try not to think about what you left at home; live in those moments with headphones on, eyes shut, thoughts focused on yourself or fun stuff coming up.

Escape to victory

Take these easy routes to freedom to restore your happy, healthy equilibrium:

Identify what you miss Nights out? Being able to eat wherever you want? Booking a spa treatment after work instead of rushing home to cook sausages and peas, again? Now, can you really no longer do these things or are you martyring yourself to the motherhood cause? I'm guessing that with a bit of planning and a blast of oomph you could reintroduce at least two of the things from your list into your repertoire, perhaps not as regularly, but occasionally for sure. Try it.

Keep a motherhood-free space in your home, even if it's just your bedside cabinet. Keep it full of things that sing to your soul and which have nothing to do with your children: a pile of favourite books, fresh flowers, bottles of essential oils, a notepad and pencil, ornaments or keepsakes that make you smile. Enforce this space fiercely, do not let others encroach on it. Once they're in, it's hard to get them out.

Set a schedule to do something small for you every day – be it a five-minute meditation or stretch session before anyone else is up, or a coffee and newspaper catch-up once you've dropped the kids off, or a bubble bath with a good novel every evening after bedtime, a ten-minute escape from the office with a podcast while you pick up your sandwich during your lunch break. Do something for you, and stick to it.

Set your ringtone and screensavers to sounds and sights that make you smile. Keep up with the latest series of your favourite show. Add new releases from your favourite author or singer to your Amazon cart.

Set yourself a self-improvement challenge This might sound like more work, but it will give your brain and self-esteem a blast of fresh air. Start an online class, get a FitBit and customise your daily sleep, steps and hydration goals, listen to a political podcast while you drive, join a book club, find a fitness app and commit to a month of ten-minute challenges.

Dig out your pre-kid jewellery box or wardrobe staples and see yourself again with fresh eyes. Push yourself out of the style rut you've been in since comfort and washability took over from flair.

Write a list of your roles, the definitions people apply to you, or which you put on yourself. Think about the list. Mama is just one of them. Think up ways to ramp up or reinstate the other sides of your life and personality.

Acknowledge that you miss your old childfree days without feeling guilt or regret, and knowing that with every year, your freedoms will be returned to you: your ability to have a bit of a lie-in when the kids learn to make their own breakfast; your ability to go to a coffee shop and read when your kids become bookworms, too; your ability to go on a weekend away with your partner when they get to the age of slumber parties. I've found the freedom from very young children has started to return, and with it a new, deeper and richer appreciation for things I once took for granted, a little discussed blessing of motherhood.

Mama says: Jessie, 43

'As soon as I became pregnant, I gave up work and wholly committed myself to being a full-time mum. A few years down the line, I felt trapped and frustrated by a life centred on my children. I love them dearly and want to do what's best for them, but I wasn't actually as good as I thought I'd be at the stay-at-home-mum lifestyle. I reached the point where I'd hold it together just about until their dad got home from work before running out of the house, not knowing where to go but knowing I had to escape. I eventually realised that, for my own sanity, I needed to go back to work, join the local tennis club and go out with friends without the children in tow.'

Prescriptions and permission slips

When you know yourself well, you are a better judge of what you need and what you don't need than any doctor or shrink. Listen to your mind and body, and write yourself a prescription or a permission slip that addresses those needs – writing it down and giving it a name will make you take it seriously, and you can then stop beating yourself up about needing a break or time out. Self-care is your best healthcare, remember! If you're feeling depleted, write yourself a 'green prescription' for a hike in the woods, or an 'Oscar prescription' for a trip to the cinema. Follow research professor Brene Brown's advice and write yourself a permission slip to take it easy, or stop being hard on yourself. If you've been run down or unwell but you have still been pushing yourself, write yourself a permission slip to 'take the time to recover'. If you've been shouting at the kids too much, write yourself a permission slip to 'take a deep breath, learn from how it made you and them feel, and move on'. Write these messages of love to yourself on Post-It notes, and stick them wherever you need reminders. Write them for your kids, as well – they might feel that they can't ask for things they clearly need, in the same way that you are unable to.

How to leave the house without the kitchen sink

One thing that puts mamas off leaving the house is the thought of all the things they need to plan, pack and lug about with them. *How can someone so small need so much*, I used to think, staring at my baby boy and the two bags I had to take everywhere. I was a woman who'd travelled Asia for three months with a small backpack, but now I needed double that to walk to a local library. Or at least I thought I did. One thing that helped when my kids were tiny and my friends and I were planning kids-dates was to stop doubling up, by sharing all the paraphernalia: someone would bring snacks, one remembered the nappies and one packed wet wipes. As they got older, and munchies became the biggest issue, I stole a friend's idea to keep a selection of non-perishable healthy treats and drinks in the boot of my car in case of emergencies. Get yourself a system early on: leaving essentials by the front door, getting a good storage bag with compartments that you refill after every trip before you're in rush mode, transferring big packets of things into portable boxes or bottles. It's also worth noting that you are not doing any long-term damage if your child gets muddy, soggy or grubby and has to stay that way until they return home. Children are also capable of entertaining themselves with sugar sachets, cups, your keys – you do not need to transport Hamley's toy department in your handbag. A scarf can act as a blanket, for nursing and a changing mat. Do not buy (excuse the pun) into the commercialism of needing countless things. 'I never had that when you were young!' grandmothers say around the country when seeing how we're weighed down, following up with a great truth: 'and it never did you any harm!'

When you leave your child with someone else

Leaving your child with anyone other than trusted family members can feel like an ordeal. I remember my first babysitter experience clearly. William was 14 months old, and we were living in Los Angeles and away from family. We needed a night out, which meant that we needed to hire a stranger, but we were nervous. We made the whole event less traumatic for us (William was oblivious) by:

- Hiring a woman who was a regular babysitter for a trusted friend. I knew she had researched and checked everything to the nth degree, and could show me references.
- Asking her to arrive after we'd fulfilled the usual bedtime routine and he was settled.
- Choosing a date spot a few minutes' walk from our house, so that we could be back quickly if we needed to be, with one of us being the designated teetotaller.
- Admitting to myself that I needed regular contact, so I didn't beat myself up for having my phone on the table and texting once an hour, something I'd forbid at family dinners normally!

Despite all these precautions, neither Russ nor I could relax, and we wolfed down our food, even forgoing our usual dessert, and literally *galloped* home. We ran, arrived panting at our front door, sweating as we stumbled into the scene: the babysitter reading a book, silence from Will's bedroom. Russ tiptoed in to check he was still there (nightmare newspaper headlines made us nervous someone might want to snatch him). He was. We paid the woman, thanked her, and promised her that if she came again next Saturday, we'd be more normal. If you're looking for a babysitter but haven't got a strong recommendation from a trusted friend, check out the apps and websites with registered babysitters who have been interviewed and checked out. Don't feel bad asking to meet first, in a public place such as a café, and asking him or her pointed questions about what he or she would do in different scenarios. Do background checks on their social media and ask for references. Do a trial run, perhaps, when you are in the house but he or she is officially in charge to see how they cope. Your child is your most treasured possession. Find the right babysitter, otherwise you won't be able to enjoy the freedom to work or play that one gives you.

Mama says: Amy, 35

'My kids don't need me any less now, as I thought they would. In fact, they really are harder work than ever. Hormones, emotions, friendships and heartaches are a whole new challenge and one which some days threatens to take me over entirely, as much as managing a newborn or teething toddler who is awake all night. Now I am awake all night worrying about them, and how they will cope with life. However, what I have now that I didn't have before, is pockets of time for myself. Time to recharge. Now they're teenagers, I can leave them alone in the house for short periods, perhaps to go out on a quick jog, pop in to see a neighbour for a coffee, or have a quick dip in the sea. These things really keep me sane. I feel that I am re-finding myself. I am reborn a new woman, much stronger for motherhood, with new passions, and new ways to cope with the chaos of life.'

The male 'babysitter'

When you need a break, please take one, and when you ask your partner, remember he is not 'babysitting' – it's his baby too! My husband has it set in stone that he goes out with his friends every Thursday, a social hour that he's held since he started working aged 21. After our children were born, this started to niggle me. Friends would also wind me up. 'Every Thursday!' they'd exclaim. 'But what about you, Sarah? What about your social life?' I went home after one particular grilling dressed up as sisterly sympathy all riled up. 'Any other night of the week!' Russ said matter-of-factly. 'I'd love you to go out with your friends any other night of the week! Six nights out of seven are free. Choose one, choose two – I like putting the kids to bed without you breathing down my neck! Just plan things!' It's amazing how his honesty switched my perspective. The 'Woe is me' became 'Wow, I'm free!' I'd been martyring myself unnecessarily, perhaps jealous that he was committed to catching up with his friends on a regular basis, while my friends and I floundered around, only setting dates for big events like a concert, or in six weeks' time. He didn't care if it was just one friend and one pint in a local pub: he was committed to Thursday. I had to learn from his social sense – and to stop thinking whether I should 'ask him to babysit' his own children. We both deserved a slice of freedom after dark; I just had to get better at achieving it.

Watch and weep

Ten films about parenthood that will make you feel less alone in your thirst for freedom:

Little Miss Sunshine	*This is 40*
Baby Boom	*Parenthood*
Matilda	*Mrs. Doubtfire*
Riding in Cars with Boys	*Captain Fantastic*
Bye Bye Love	*Mr. Mom*

You need to get out more

The most claustrophobic element of motherhood for many of us is the repetitiveness: the *Groundhog Day* dullness of every hour, day, week following the same strict code, an endless list of thankless tasks. There is no doubt: motherhood can make us feel boring and trapped. A recent BBC News programme revealed how it was these feelings that led many British women to regret having children, one mother telling host Victoria Derbyshire 'life shouldn't be about giving up your life, your freedom, so they can have a life', another saying she 'begrudged [her children's] intrusion on her time'. British women are not alone. In 2016 a German survey by YouGov showed that 8 per cent of the 1,200 women interviewed regretted becoming parents, and one of the main reasons was their loss of freedom.

Escape the prison:

- Adapt your old social life to your new responsibilities. Just because you can't bar hop anymore, it doesn't mean that you can't see your friends. Host more girls' nights at your home. Get everyone to bring something to eat or drink so that you don't feel the pressure of providing it all.
- Instead of trying out fancy new restaurants for dinner, try their breakfast or brunch menu with friends who have kids. Get dressed up like it's a night out. Take colouring books and set realistic expectations about the amount of time you'll be able to talk.
- Get help. Join a gym or a yoga studio that offers free childcare.
- Put events that are important to you in your diary. It's amazing the lift having something to look forward to will give you – so book theatre tickets, a spa appointment, a night away.
- Resume a hobby you once loved and can do from home: painting, sewing, soup making, origami, Sudoku, and so on. Make a night of the week your 'crochet night', for example, and tell your partner that they are in charge. Make yourself deaf to demands they can handle, pour yourself a tea or a glass of prosecco, and lose your mind to creativity.
- Outsource the jobs that really make you mad. Get your

shopping delivered from your local supermarket, ask your babysitter to iron your shirts once the kids are asleep (or only buy non-crease clothes), set up automatic delivery of household items on Amazon, buy a slow cooker so that your meals virtually take care of themselves. Our generation are so lucky to have so much external help that comes at little financial cost but gives us huge mental gains.

- Make the monotonous chores more fun: plug in headphones and listen to the book you've been meaning to read, dance to your favourite band's new album, catch up with a friend on the phone while you're sorting laundry. Time will fly and your sense of achievement will soar.

- Push yourself to go out even when you're tired or stressed and want to hibernate. You'll never regret quality time with a good friend. Have an invigorating shower, pop on some makeup, listen to upbeat tunes while you get dressed – you'll feel pleased that you made the effort rather than wimping out.

- Introduce the kids to things that make you feel free. Go on a hike – just an easier one than you would have done without them. Take them to the cinema, as long as the film is appropriate. Book a holiday abroad – one that has family activities. Visit a museum, and pick up the family fun sheet. Accommodate your kids, and teach them how to accommodate you.

Let Mother Nature share your motherload

Nothing blows away the cobwebs of claustrophobia like getting outdoors and into nature, but a recent study highlighted the sad truth that the average American adult spends more time in a vehicle than in fresh air each day, and British grown-ups can't be far behind. It's even worse for children. The Dirt is Good: Free the Children campaign (backed by the National Institute of Play) conducted a study of 12,000 parents across ten countries and uncovered that youngsters in America spent less time outside each day than prisoners and free-range chickens – and Brits were going the same way. We can see this from the empty parks and playgrounds we drive past daily. Not only is this devastating for children, who learn to be brave, imaginative and kind through communicating with Mother Nature, but it's also bad for frazzled parents, too. Moving meltdowns, tantrums and the feeling of being trapped into the Great Outdoors is always a good thing for everyone. No drama feels as huge or significant when faced with the beauty of the world around us. Prioritising parenting *en plein-air* can save your vocal cords – and furniture – and bring harmony, tidiness and connection into a family home. It blows away cobwebs and gives us an instant boost of awe and gratitude.

This might sound schmaltzy but an unignorable amount of research has been done into the significant mental, social, physical and emotional benefits of spending more time outside, in fresh air, with free play and a sense of freedom. A recent study of 18,500 people conducted by the University of Derby and the Wildlife Trust showed that there was a scientifically significant increase in people's health and happiness when a connection to nature and active nature behaviours, such as feeding birds and planting flowers for bees, was sustained over a period of months. Research demonstrates that children exposed to the natural world show increases in self-esteem, as getting outside teaches them how to take risks, unleash their creativity and gives them a chance to exercise, play, and discover without restrictions.

Not only are there emotional and psychological advantages

to playing outside, but there are physical advantages, too. Obviously, if a child is playing outside, she will be way more physically fit than the child that stays indoors, sitting and gawping at a television or an iPad screen on a sofa, but the great thing about this is that it can have long-lasting effects, as proven by a study in the *International Journal of Obesity* by an Australian team of nutritionists and academics. Years down the road, the child will still be more active and less likely to be over-weight. If you think about this, it makes perfect sense: teach a child when they're young to love moving around the outdoors and they will love it – and move – forever. Nervous for the future but prompted by studies like this, the NHS has released new guidelines regarding children and activity, suggesting that kids aged between five and 18 should get at least one hour of activity outside every day, and giving a stern warning to parents that the sedentary, indoor lifestyle children are currently living can lead to serious problems later in life, such as heart disease and type-2 diabetes.

Feel free as a bird

The importance of getting children, and myself, out into nature was probably the first lesson I learnt as a parent. I became a mother at the same time as a dear friend, a Norwegian girl living near me, who insisted that instead of spending those early foggy mornings of nursing in coffee shops we walked in local parks. 'There is no such thing as bad weather, just bad clothing,' Solveig reminded me if ever I texted her with predictions of rain. And we walked, our babies snoozing in the fresh air, our spirits lifted by the boost of vitamin D and cardiovascular pumping, my stress levels slumping when faced with blossoming trees and chirping birds. I set myself the goal then: to always live as a parent with the outdoors as our biggest source of entertainment. If nothing else, it is so much cheaper than lugging offspring to those indoor play centres, and the chances are much less of catching some ghastly bug or getting set on by a teething toddler. In nature, you can make the rules of engagement: play games, sing songs, I've even used the time to get my kids interested in meditation and yoga. Fresh air and unstructured play have built confidence in my two, and encouraged their imagination remarkably. Being out in the wild with friends has also taught them to negotiate (big sticks are a valuable commodity in our local playground), to be coura-geous (climbing a tree that looked out of reach, falling out of it and getting a scrape but carrying on), and to work as a team (it's so funny to see these busy elves pulling together to build a fort, make a nest or dig a hole). They learn more in these all-weather hours about how to be a good human than when I'm sitting over them with a beady-eye, making sure they've done their home-work or practised the drums.

Liberty for all!

How do we, as busy and stressed – and, let's not forget, exhausted – parents do this? How do we drag our kids outside when their screen addiction (and ours) is making the house look extra inviting, or they stare skywards and moan about ominous clouds or needing snacks? Bribes work. Bribes are good. For Mother Nature, a mum can use some tricks. Mine include, but are not limited to, outdoor toys such as bubble mixture (never underestimate the power of bubble blowing and popping), kites and streamers, a kid-friendly magnifying glass for bug watching, a toy tea-set and a picnic hamper filled with favourite treats, and a book about rocks (my children are currently obsessed with geodes) for some geeking out among pebbles and boulders.

The biggest trick though, of course, is *engaging* with them! Leave your phone at home. Look at them, get down in the dirt and play. Get to know their friends, join them in a race, act as excited as you possibly can when they discover a funny-looking leaf or present you with a flower. Your positive energy will feed them, which will feed you. A sad truth of modern motherhood is that our faces – the face that no one loves more and knows more than our offspring – is often hidden from their view by a device, our minds stolen from them by our Facebook feeds. I am addicted to my phone. I realise it and acknowledge it and have set myself an allotted amount of time on it during the day, and I am not allowed to look at it from when I pick up the kids until their bed-time, or at weekends when we are having outdoor time in a park, forest or at the beach. And it's worth it, because I get to see their faces as they see the world, giving me the pleasure of seeing the world in a new, surprising way.

This is the true gift given to us by Mother Nature. When children are given time to settle into her warm embrace, something magical happens. The natural urge we are all born with to explore, admire and build takes over and mamas become adventurers, risk-takers and caretakers alongside their kids. We jump in waves, jump in puddles, jump in piles of golden autumnal leaves, and jump into fresh air and freedom. We return to the cocoon of our home happy, dirty, with muscles used and brains buzzing, the claustrophobia of the day-to-day parenting grin aired and rinsed – all thanks to the best free fun a family can enjoy.

Your PG rating

Under each P or G, list your personal priorities and answers to revisit in times of need!

The Ps:
Purpose To stop feeling trapped by your role as a mother.
Perspective Your family won't fall apart if you take some time for yourself, you know that!
Presence If you make 'me time' you'll value your 'we time' more.

The Gs:
Gratitude You are thankful for the moments of space you get – even the five minutes to drink a coffee. You have learnt to cherish time and peace in a new way since becoming a mama.
Goals Set time for friends and hobbies, or time to introduce your family to things you've always loved.
Going for it Book three fun dates into your diary – today!

TAKE A DEEP BREATH, MAMA

Find George Michael's 'Freedom '90' video on YouTube or GooglePlay. Turn it up. Own the room or own the car. Think about the lyrics. Think about the you that you've always been. Think about what makes you *feel alive*. Forget about the laundry. Forget about tomorrow's conference call. Forget about the PTA fundraiser. Forget about dinner. For the next few minutes just dance and tell yourself that you will not give up on yourself, and what makes you feel free.

4

Learn to Love Your Body

It was a few years into motherhood that I realised that my body no longer felt like my own. It had become a scaffold, a tree trunk, a climbing frame, a pillowy trampoline – solid and grounded, yet wobbly in places, a safe haven for my children to spring from and jump off. Even my husband stopped seeing me for the woman he fell in love with. At times I felt he recognised me only as a reliable machine that ran the family: a fleshy robot with car keys, wet wipes and reusable shopping bags. When I finished nursing Matilda and the last visible, physical tug of corporeal servitude to motherhood was sent out for pasture, my breasts dried up but I still felt forever physically changed. But changed how?

Do you look different? Right then, I have something for you to think about. Do you *have* to see these changes in appearance as negative, or actually, are they positive? When I sat and analysed my reaction to my new post-baby body, I saw that although

I was squidgier and droopier than I would have liked, and the stretch marks weren't fading fast enough for my liking, I had a new respect for myself and my body. It had produced and fed two growing children. It had carried me through the trauma of three miscarriages to allow me to deliver two healthy babies. It had kept going on little, and sometimes no, sleep, and given me enough resilience to care for sick children without catching the same bug.

Going through this fundamental physical change also allowed me to take a wider view on bodies and how we as society want them to look. A woman's body is prodded and poked so much during the pregnancy and birth process that you have to release a level of shame or embarrassment that might have clouded your self-worth before. How can we worry about soft corners or rounded bellies when a miracle has taken place within us? The best thing I ever did was to stop caring about my cellulite. I wore white leggings at a 5k fun run last week. I jiggled, but I giggled.

Body-positivity pointers

We all have bad days when we're feeling super lethargic, or we can't take our hand out of the family-sized packet of crisps, or we catch an unflattering glimpse of our chin and feel desperately sad. Instant ways to make you feel beautiful, or to understand why you feel bad, can include:

- Getting to know and understand your menstrual cycle. Once I started keeping track of my period, I started to recognise that I'd feel low, chubby and bloated, and find it hard to sleep, for one week of the month. This was due to hormonal changes in my body, which were somewhat out of my control, rather than a true reflection of what was happening to me because I was lazy or unhealthy.

Knowing this didn't stop the negative feelings, but it made me remember that they were temporary and that I should give myself a break because the rollercoaster ride a woman's hormones puts her on every month is serious stuff.

- Treating yourself to a nice rub-down with a body cream or oil that rehydrates and helps stretch marks.
- Repeating to yourself, 'My body made a baby, my body is carrying me through this part of my life, my body is remarkable,' and actually appreciating that in the grand scheme of what you are, and what you have done, a few wobbles are irrelevant.
- Taking a little longer than usual to shower, and scrubbing away bad feelings with an exfoliator.
- Stopping for a long, hard look in the mirror. Find things you *do* like about your appearance. Stop mean thoughts, and express contentment with your pretty eyes or new haircut.
- Taking action and removing remnants of rough days that make you feel frumpy or guilty. Get rid of dried-up old makeup and baggy clothes. Five minutes of housekeeping will reframe your mood.

A-list lies and un-reality shows

Newspapers and magazines love to talk about women's bodies. I know. When I was the editor-in-chief of one of the US's biggest celebrity weeklies, I relied on the fact that on a quiet news week I could prop up sales with a baby bump or radical diet cover story. Women love to read about other women's body battles and secrets – and they love to see photos. But do these stories make us feel less alone, or are they dwindling away our self-worth? The language used in the media about a woman's body 'snapping back into shape after birth' or 'beating the baby bulge' can promote feelings of unworthiness. *If she can drop ten pounds in ten weeks why can't I? I'm a loser.* I've been around enough celebrities to know that (a) they either feel the same as any other woman (vulnerable, judged, bloated); or (b) they've got to a place where they don't care and are using their bodies along with their voices to try to change the public dialogue. Don't get sucked into your newsfeed and feel bad about yourself. Turn it off and head to a local swimming pool instead. Witness bodies of all shapes and sizes and softness ploughing through water, pulling themselves out, diving off the side, supporting children. And don't fall into the trap of jealously bitching over a celebrity's thighs. You are better than that. Listen to the positive voices (P!nk, Stacey Solomon, Fearne Cotton and Kelly Clarkson are great mum voices to listen to) and do understand, it's easier to 'snap back into shape' when you are having secret surgery and are swallowing weight-loss pills – and you have the money to recruit a personal chef, personal trainer and a full-time nanny. You, my dear, should only be in competition with your best self, which means choosing foods that make you feel strong and sated, and setting your own goals with the scales. Concentrate on being the best version of you, not a poor version of a Z-lister.

The weight debate

Yes, there are sags, bags and bits that drag, we wiggle and jiggle, and feel different in our skin, but the questions over how we ditch the weight that we've put on during pregnancy has become too big a deal, right? The healthiest way to lose weight isn't to measure yourself against an unachievable ideal, but to think about feeling comfortable in your clothes. Rather than hitting a number on the scales, aim to get back into your pre-pregnancy wardrobe, and don't be harsh or hard on yourself to the point of hurting your physical or mental health. Follow a diet plan that is good for you. Don't starve yourself. You'll end up weak and miserable, and eating sugary treats to keep going. And you need to eat enough to care for your child, and to produce milk if you're breastfeeding. Keep sated between meals – and keep your blood sugar levels balanced – by eating high-fibre snacks such as wholemeal bread, crackers and raisins. Don't dis nutrients. Your body has been through a lot. Rebuild it with iron, protein and calcium, and keep it healthy with vitamins and minerals. 'Eat the rainbow' was a piece of advice I was given, which helped me to remember to chow down on a good cross-section of replenishing foods.

Even when you are at a weight you are happy with, you need to maintain a healthy relationship with food. You should be focused on being healthy as much as being slim, so avoid empty calories (fizzy drinks, alcohol, crisps) that do nothing to boost your body, and go for fats that are good for you, such as nuts and avocados. Foods with a high water content help to suppress your appetite, so salads and soups can be added to meals or used as snacks to help you feel full for longer.

A body of contrasts

You also need to exercise your honesty muscle. On some premenstrual days I can't stay away from the biscuits in the cupboard, so allow myself to dive in. When I go back home to England, I know that I'm going to put on weight eating all the favourite food that I can't find in my new country of America (I had fish and chips four days in a row last summer) and feel heavier on the flight back. At Hallowe'en, I know I'm going to raid my kids' trick-or-treat candy stash like a sneaky goblin. At

Christmas, when you can't swing an elf without landing on a platter of sweet delights, I know I'm going to gorge on sugar. I know it. I enjoy it. I savour every bite as I feel my jeans tighten and know that I'll get back on track when this unusual period ends. I am mindful of treating myself, and I don't hide it or feel guilty about it. I choose to eat badly in some moments, but I choose to be healthy and sensible mostly. Give yourself a break when you're feeling festive, or hormonal, or know that a slice of cake will soothe your soul and make your day easier. I've found keeping a note about my weight (I jump on the scales once a week) keeps me aware without becoming obsessed.

Food for thought for busy mamas

- Pack snacks to avoid hunger attacks: balance your blood sugar with a handful of nuts, hardboiled eggs, apple slices coated in almond butter or a scoop of hummus and carrots. Being prepared will keep you from crashing and reaching for a tray of doughnuts.
- Have easy, healthy lunches and dinners stockpiled. Buying a slow cooker was the best thing I ever did apart from having my children. I can chuck healthy ingredients into the pot as I'm drinking my breakfast coffee and come home eight hours later to a delicious-smelling home and dinner for two nights.
- Stay hydrated. Our bodies are made up of 70 per cent water, and we need it to keep everything flowing and moving. Start carrying a water bottle around with you, or force yourself to have a glass before you do anything else in the morning. Two litres a day is a good goal to set yourself.

▶

- You're not always hungry. Before you eat other than at mealtimes, ask yourself why. Mostly, when I'm supposed to be working and I start scrounging around the fridge, it's because I'm bored or tired. For many people, when they feel hunger it's actually thirst, so try satisfying the craving with a herbal tea, sparkling water or a cup of coffee before snacking.
- Never shop on an empty stomach. You'll be tempted to snap up naughty foods and spend too much money. Crunch a pear en route, or have a cup of tea before you go.
- Keep easy-to-reach, nutritious elements in the kitchen cupboard for making into meals. Beans, nuts, seeds, porridge oats, flaxseeds and garlic are easy-to-store power-foods, full of benefits.
- Keep an eye on your iron. Too little of it and you might feel fatigued and lacklustre. Great iron sources include nuts, spinach, dried apricots, potatoes, lean meats and eggs.
- Chill out. If you are desperate for a humongous slice of cake, don't worry about it. If you know a sugary snack is on the cards, and three pounds of celery and a vat of asparagus soup won't scratch the itch, be honest with yourself and revel in every bite.

Mama does *not* need a cocktail!

We mamas are being overloaded with messages telling us that booze will make the mummy journey so much easier. T-shirts, wine glasses, GIFs and quotes – for some reason social media and clever marketeers (and fellow mums) are pushing the idea that we can find solutions at the bottom of a bottle. Before you jump on board, as I did when I first became a parent and searched for salvation from tiredness, boredom and frustration in a glass or two of prosecco, know the facts. An occasional glass of something stronger that coffee is a treat, a quick relaxer and a way to socially bond with friends. But alcohol is a toxin, a depressant, it makes you more tired and unable to drive, and if you're concerned with losing weight, it is just a glass of empty calories. I've seen friends fall for the 'mummy deserves a happy hour to make it till bedtime' trap or the 'cool mamas do Shiraz on the shelf, not elf on the shelf' lie, and the self-loathing that they feel and the danger they put their families in is not fun. Think before you drink. Indulge occasionally if you want to, but look for healthier ways to de-stress and hang out with friends other than having alcohol as your default setting.

Adoption: the mind–body connection

The media and mothers focus a lot on how to accept your new body after childbirth, but women who have adopted a child need to adapt, too. Not only perhaps to the feelings of deep frustration and sadness when they couldn't conceive, or they decided it wasn't right for their body, but also afterwards, when strangers could question their physical bond or ask where their child got their looks from, or why they chose to adopt a child so different in appearance to themselves, if that is the case. There is also the regret of not being able to breastfeed the child that could cause some physical longing, or a fear for genetic features of their baby that they would not be able to understand. My friends who have adopted children wish everyone to know that they feel no different from mothers who gave birth: the connection is as visceral and emotional. To doubt that their child is *their* child is monstrous.

Mama says: Emily, 42

'My mummy guilt came after we brought our son Zac home from China. I'd always known I would adopt, and after a year of stress and paperwork we finally had our little boy home. But as meaningful as that was, I still had meals to prepare for my kids, laundry, cleaning, errands ... I started to feel tremendous guilt whenever I became impatient or frustrated or needed time alone. This was guilt that I had not felt with my biological daughter. This sweet boy had travelled so far, separated from birth parents and caretakers, endured surgeries, and I'm exasperated because I'm unable to have a conversation with anyone at a party because I needed to keep up with my active 18-month-old. Perhaps I don't deserve such a special boy. Am I being a better mum than his birth mother in China would have been? Does he feel my love in a way that makes him whole? I had to let go of that guilt for my son. It's unrealistic for us to never feel those emotions; parenting is hard work. He's my son, I'm his mum, we both get upset at times, but we laugh, kiss and hug much more often.'

Teach your child body confidence

Instilling in your child the ability to accept their bodies is one of your greatest responsibilities. A child whose mother is always trying to hide her sticky-out ears could grow up paranoid about her physical appearance. A child whose mother laughed at her chubby thighs might grow up with a strange relationship to food. How do we teach our children to be strong, fit and energetic and to make good food choices without making them too self-aware about everything they eat and every calorie they burn? This isn't just a daughter issue; this is a son issue too. We need to be mindful of how we talk about our bodies in front of everyone.

1. **First and foremost**, emulate how you want them to feel. This could help you, too. Stop looking at yourself with a judgemental eye, stop using negative language when talking about your body. Forget the cruel things your mother or friends, or so-called-friends, have made you feel self-conscious about in the past. Focus on your body from a health perspective. 'Mummy is eating more vegetables and fruits because they are super-foods which will make my skin glow,' is preferable for your child to hear than, 'I've eaten too much sugar today. I feel gross. I'm going to break out in spots because I did that!' Don't ever look in the mirror with a grimace and say, 'What a lard arse!'; look in the mirror and say, 'Girl, you are fine' (finger clicking acceptable as you do this). Only talk about body shape and weight or diets in positive discussions about making good choices.

2. **Highlight the power and wonder of bodies** Play in a way that encourages movement and expression – we love a dance party in my house. Play team games, run races, notice when a child does something using their strength or mobility, or with grace, and lavish them with praise. Pay attention when they tell you about their PE class or basketball game, ask them to recreate moments so that you can see. Tell them how proud and impressed you are. Talk about your childhood and what you liked to play.

3. **Teach them about their bodies** and how they work: why they poo, why their brain remembers certain things, what their skeleton does. Tell them how much they've grown that year; perhaps keep a wall chart or a journal with a graph in it, and which immunisations they've had and why. Help them to take care of their bodies,

explaining the importance of cleaning their teeth, washing their hair, eating vegetables.

4. **Nurture them inside and out** Say nice things about how they look. Point out family traits and resemblances. Make sure that they get enough sleep, enough water, enough vitamins through their diet or with supplements. Help them to repair hurt feelings if someone has said something mean about their appearance by listening to them, soothing them with a hug, and sharing stories about how you built your resilience in similarly trying times.

5. **Answer any questions they have** as honestly and scientifically as possible. Yes, I've had period conversations with my son when he's caught me weeing and been confused by the 'weird little nappy' I'm wearing. If you talk without drama, they will hopefully be able to carry an honest, open, non-gender specific attitude to their body and health into adulthood.

The cover-up conundrum

My children often walk in when I'm having a bath. For some reason my five-year-old finds it the perfect time to go to the loo, and my seven-year-old – who rarely tells me anything about his day, his friends or his feelings when I ask – finds this the perfect time to download his deepest thoughts. When they see me in all my naked glory, they will ask questions about pubic hair, stretch marks, where they came out of, and make general comments about my shape and size. I've learnt to be more than fine with it – if they can't see their mum and ask her questions about bodies, who *can* they ask? – but

I have been thinking about when it becomes inappropriate. Is there an age at which we have to cover up? Is there an age when it becomes damaging? I know through playground discussions that this is a hot point of discussion in many school-age children's homes and I have come to the conclusion that this is something for an individual family to decide. I run a naked house so that no one ever feels that there is anything wrong or shameful about my body or theirs, so I can give them a live biology lesson about women's bodies and how all bodies age and change, but this is too much for some mamas or their offspring. I'd say, focus on your comfort level: if someone wants to cover up, let them. If a child wants to be more private, allow them to be. Most kids develop their own sense of modesty as pre-teens, and it is important for them to set their personal boundaries around privateness and demureness, so allow them to say 'privacy, please' and respect their wishes. Allow them to close the door when they're getting dressed. Stop roaming around naked, but don't get flustered if they walk in on you naked. We've also taught our kids that although it is okay if mummy or daddy helps them out of the bath, or puts cream on their body, or for a doctor to look at your privates if mummy or daddy is in the room, no one else should look at, or ask to look at, or touch, their privates.

The power of touch

A hug or kiss can give children a physical and mental boost when they are feeling worn-down or defeated. In these busy days, we sometimes feel guilty about just being, sitting and snuggling, but we shouldn't. Evidence tells us that these low-key moments of connection have huge benefits. Every Sunday morning, the kids climb into my husband's and my bed for a group hug and discussion about the day ahead before we start breakfast. We adults get as big a boost from this closeness as the kids do. Why?

- Touch is a language that allows us to communicate acceptance, love and understanding without saying a word.
- Touch from a trusted loved one can give stress and pain relief to an anxious child, and comfort to their parent. A hug a day keeps us calm and builds trust.
- Touch is a bonding action and reduces anxiety – one reason why 'skin to skin' (where a baby is held naked against the mother's skin) is such a crucial part of the mother–baby experience immediately after childbirth.
- Research shows that children from households where hugs and kisses and holding hands are part of day-to-day life display less violent or aggressive behaviour towards others than those who don't.
- Daily small gestures – a ruffle of hair, a high five, a pat on the back – signal solidarity, attachment and positive energy. They build team spirit in a family and between friends.

Let's get physical: exercise while parenting

I am a woman more naturally disposed to sitting on her bottom with a book than working out, but the truth is, exercise is one of those things – perhaps the only one – that you'll never regret doing. However tired you feel going to a gym, you will always leave uplifted, energised and rejuvenated. Just this morning, I wanted to drink coffee and bunk-off my weekly yoga class, but I remembered the sense of accomplishment and community that came with the physical boost and got my sorry ass to class. Zero regrets. Since becoming a mother, I have got myself into a healthier routine by telling myself it didn't have to be an ordeal, that it could be a short spurt, not a long drag. Twenty crunches while I waited for a kettle to boil was doable. I could stretch in the shower while my hair conditioner soaked in. Once you start moving your body, you want to continue – it's just the start that is hard. I downloaded motivational apps on to my phone, and found an army of supporters who wanted to see me get fitter with no judgement. I bought myself a pair of good trainers. I used a long power walk as a chance to listen to new audiobooks or to call my mum. When my kids were very young and I couldn't get out of the house, I found yoga videos on YouTube to stretch and eighties videos to make me hop. A skipping rope and a mini trampoline are reasonable gifts you can give to your thighs.

Make love or make dinner?

Before our stressful conception chapter began, however irritated I was with my husband (he pretends to be deaf to avoid my instructions and has the memory of a goldfish), I still found him irresistible, to the point of being a sex pest. Oh, how the times have changed since becoming a mother! Friends have whispered that the same thing has happened to them. A separate bedroom with a stack of Elena Ferrante novels on the bedside cabinet sounds sexier than a heaving husband and an orgasm. I don't think it's *just* that I'm tired all the time, because I can still partake in my other favourite energetic hobbies with abandon (stockpiling Ferrero Rocher, crucifying country music ballads at karaoke and grape-vining to the Spice Girls). It's that I feel less sexy, and therefore want less sex. My hormones are disrupted, my mind elsewhere. My husband was relieved, at first, that he now got to watch *Match of the Day* without me gyrating in an unalluring manner in front of the television, and I didn't even notice at first.

A physical connection is important in a healthy relationship, however. Intimacy and pleasure are two things you can only get from each other, and that makes your bond unique. Without sensuality, you're just roommates. Mentally, a loving sex life correlates with overall happiness in a relationship, thanks to the hormones that flush your bodies during the act. Dopamine, released during sex, gives you both a shot of easy, free and safe joy. Orgasm brings on a release of endorphins, which make you feel relaxed and contented. And a recent study published in *Personality and Social Psychology Bulletin* revealed that the mental uptick you get from sex lasts for up to 24 hours. An increase in good, regular sex also boosts self-esteem and self-confidence, which feeds your glow in all areas of your life, and promotes a loving, intimate relationship beyond the bedroom.

There are physical health benefits, too. Not only will sex burn calories and burn fat, but it also boosts your antibodies, which makes you more resistant to colds and flu. Sex helps you sleep better, and better sleep builds your immune system. Oxytocin, which is released during orgasm, reduces stress, lowers cortisol levels, and helps to soothe pain, and women who have regular sex report having lighter periods and fewer cramps. Sex also lowers blood pressure. Feeling saucy yet?

How to get your groove back

You can rebuild your mojo among the mayhem and maternity underwear.

- Take the pressure off: start slow and easy. Aim for intimacy and focus on each other. You'll remember how nice it feels to be close.
- Swap your ugly, industrial-sized bra and big pants for a pretty set. Do this for you; he is secondary but will like it too.
- Get your partner to make you dinner, while you take a

bath, then eat together, leisurely, with the kids tucked
away in bed.

- Flicking through photo albums of when you first met will
reignite a spark and lots of sensual memories.
- Stay in a hotel for a night (come on, grandparents –
babysit!) and set yourself the rule that you can only talk
about the children for the first hour, then kid convo is
off limits.
- Go to the gym together. Building up a sweat can be erotic.
- Read erotic literature in bed, or watch a sexy film (*Betty
Blue*, *Eyes Wide Shut*, and *Body Heat*).
- Go to see a rock concert together. You'll feel young and
carefree, and you're already sweaty so . . .
- Massage. Either take it in turns to rub each other down,
or get a couple's massage at a spa.
- Try him telling you you're the best mother in the world,
taking the baby out for a few hours, while you sleep, and
then returning with a sleeping baby and an adoring look
in his eye.

Spice rack

Sometimes we have to use more than Mother Nature gave
us, and when two new parents are tired, groggy and craving
a *The Crown* marathon, relying on naked flesh and a double
bed won't be enough to get things hot. Natural spice can be
added with aphrodisiacs. Chilli releases endorphins, its heat
giving us swollen lips and flushed skin, two visible signs of
sexual desire. Cinnamon heats up your body temperature, as
does ginger. Cardamom increases heart rate and blood flow.
Chuck these in your dinner and get your appetite back.

Mama says: Becci, 39

'Sharing our bed with Sam was one of the most special times with our new son. We put rails on the bed, bought him a special co-sleeping crib, and stared in wonder at him as he dozed off between us. It made nursing much easier. I didn't have to stagger through chilly, dark hallways and sit on the floor in his room. Yes, sex was an issue – neither of us wanted to do it in bed while he was in there with us. But when we were in the mood, we made love on the floor in the lounge. It actually made things a bit more exciting. We hadn't had sex anywhere other than the bedroom for years and we felt like sneaky teenagers again.'

The affection anchor

If you are still not persuaded, or you feel unable, to have sex, remember that there are other ways to be intimate that cement your bond and give you something to hang on to until full-throttle passion returns. If you're just not in a mental or physical space to make sex a priority – you might have postnatal depression, or you think it might hurt after a difficult delivery or a C-section – know that you are not alone, that your doctor or midwife may be able to offer you solutions, and your partner should be supportive rather than pushy until you are ready. Until you are ready, do know that many of the benefits of sex can be experienced just through loving connections like kissing, hugging, a hand on the back, watching television snuggled close or holding hands. It is the affection between a pair that is so powerful, more than the sex itself, so work on maintaining, or rebuilding, your warmth as a couple.

Will he still love me tomorrow?

We're not supposed to admit it in this age of equality but many of us mothers worry about the effect our changing moods and appearance will have on our partner, especially physically. 'Will he still fancy me?' is a cry that ricochets around a playground when a new mum contemplates her swinging, lumpy boobs and stretch marks with other mum friends. The answer is simple: if you've got yourself a good one, not only will he still fancy you but he will also be in awe of you. As you pull yourself back together at your own pace as well as getting more comfortable in your own skin and more confident in your own appearance, he will admire you: 'She did that?!', 'She carried my child, gave birth to it, nourished it, and she carries it around to a bundle of mind-numbing classes and play dates!'

I have these results from a very quick survey of ten dad friends: 100 per cent of them don't think about your stretch marks, cellulite or wobbly bits, they just love having sex with you. If your partner is being mean about your appearance, it says more about him than you. He needs to shape up mentally more than you need to shape up physically! If his criticism comes from a place of his own body insecurity, get fit together, eat well together, make each other feel special (physically and emotionally) and let him worship you. You deserve it.

Beautifying down below

After giving birth, many of my friends who've had vaginal deliveries have said that their pussy is less the cat's meow and more like a dog's dinner. There are bits popping out where they shouldn't be and random things hanging down. One friend's husband told her, as she cradled her newborn in her arms, that the experience of watching his daughter arrive was like watching his favourite pub burn down: his safe haven had disappeared forever, and even if it was rebuilt, it wouldn't have the same atmosphere. She somehow refrained from slapping him (he probably has the overriding effects of the epidural to thank for that), but she did feel self-conscious and avoided having sex with him for the next 12 months (which probably hurt him more than a slap, anyway).

The key thing to remember is that your vagina is elastic and resilient and was built for the task of giving birth. Although it might look different, the sensations for you and your husband will be very similar to what they were pre-baby, unless there has been serious trauma during delivery which needs to be addressed by your doctor – and don't be embarrassed to do so. Try daily Kegel exercises while you're brushing your teeth. The first few attempts at sex might feel sore and awkward, so it's important to do just what you feel comfortable doing. Make lube your friend. Light some candles. Focus on what feels good and familiar rather than what feels weird and different.

Mama says: Verity, 37

'Don't just assume that everything down there is healing up nicely. If you feel any kind of pain or weirdness, don't ignore it – get it checked out. I'm quite shy and prudish, but when an itching and discomfort didn't subside after six months, I got out a mirror and checked myself out. It looked all wrong – and it was. I had ripped so badly that I had needed a lot of stitches, and I'd ended up with two small holes instead of one expanding one. That was why sex hurt so badly. I had surgery and everything was fine – and we've gone on to have another baby – but don't ignore your instincts.'

Your PG rating

Note, score and plan your family's priorities (using these key words to give you structure) going forward.

The Ps:
Purpose To live your healthiest life, inside and out.
Perspective You have the willpower and fortitude to make productive changes.
Presence You are strong, resilient and beautiful, and you are kind to your body and mind.

The Gs:
Gratitude Be thankful for the body that you've been given and what it has done.
Goals To keep your body healthy and strong, and to encourage your children to do the same.
Going for it Make healthy choices and beneficial changes, starting today.

TAKE A DEEP BREATH, MAMA

Close your eyes and go back in time. You are growing your baby in your belly. The blood is rushing around both your bodies, feeding you both, making you strong. Your baby arrives. Your arms hold him close and safe, your breast is the perfect resting place, your breath mingles with his, your eyes absorb your creation. You did this. You built this. You will protect this child for as long as you can. Your body is a temple of strength, a fortress to unconditional love. Isn't it incredible what we can do?

5

Understand Your Mama Brain

'Mothers are all slightly insane'
J.D. Salinger, The Catcher in the Rye

You might read the above quote by Salinger and think, as I did, (a) how rude! (b) how true! and (c) how necessary, because if we mamas didn't embrace our battiness, we would collapse. I've definitely become more eccentric since becoming a mother. I wouldn't have gone out in public in my pyjamas before (now, I have a needs-must attitude to that), I wouldn't have imagined publicly shouting 'Please don't throw earwigs at your friends' or 'No, you've listened to the fart song twice now, that's enough!' would have even been in my vocabulary, and that doing so would cause zero embarrassment. I certainly wouldn't have imagined that pretending to be a tickle monster, or dressing up as Alice in Wonderland in my forties, or spending my Friday nights working in an imaginary hat shop in my son's bedroom would fill my heart with everything and more. These are all clear signs that I have lost my former sense of decorum – and it feels wonderfully liberating.

Getting into a Zen mindset

Let's revisit the guiding principles of being a Zen mama outlined in the Introduction: increasing your ability to be present in the moment, trusting your gut, silencing your inner critic, and learning to ignore outside influences, finding time to be happy and to relax, and seeking authenticity, and finding your own route to calmness and contentment, these are all cornerstones of finding your rhythm and joy as a mama. The chores and hassles of everyday parenthood can be reinterpreted as exercises in gratitude. You have to wake up early *because* you have children who know that they can rely on you. Life is noisy *because* it is full of people and places to go to. Your children are constantly asking you questions and talking your ear off *because* their brains are growing and full of excitement. There is laundry, housework and the supermarket shopping to do, *because* you have a home that you are making safe, warm and happy for your family. You fall into bed sore and tired every night *because* you've been there for your children and *because* you've been using your body and brain to make everything work. *Because* you are alive!

Roadblocks and speed bumps

There will always – *always!* – be times when it is impossible to live in such a careful, contemplative way. Your schedule is crammed, you're juggling a million invites and requests, you've let healthy habits slide and you can't remember the last time you did something just for *you*. Kids scream and whine, partners don't listen, people are rude … oh I get it! Some days I find it easy to be all mystical and monkish like my Zen role model Thomas Merton, other days I do a great impression of

Miss Hannigan from *Annie*, hiding from my offspring in a hot bath behind a slammed door. I can look positively like Edvard Munch's *The Scream* if I have to ask them five times to stop playing drums on the back of my car seat, but I do try to be better. I've discovered over my seven-plus years of parenting that shouting and storming off does little for anyone's mood except heighten feelings of upset, guilt and drama.

Hit the reset button on your brain when you've had enough:

Remember that every day is a new day Put yesterday's drama behind you. Put the tantrum from five minutes ago behind you – yours or theirs! If you feel that you have something to apologise to your children for, explain and say sorry, think about why you did what you did, then move on. Don't let it worm away at your brain so that you then feel compelled to over-compensate or let them get away with things they shouldn't.

Ask for help at home School-age children are more capable than you think, and will enjoy feeling useful and challenged if you ask them to clean their room, get their own drinks, make their bed. Make a wall chart to reward them for completing small, age-appropriate tasks.

Write IOUs with friends – swap one school drop-off for a pick-up, take it in turns to buy joint teacher gifts, set a regular play-date schedule that gives you and your mama friend a few extra hours of peace.

Cherish future plans, reminisce about past events. Thinking forward to something special I have organised with my family, and thinking back to a time when someone did something kind for me, puts a spring in my step.

Get the vibe right – are you really anxious and stressed, or are you excited? When I have a lot on my plate (kids parties to plan, visitors coming to stay, events to get to, girl time to squeeze in), and my brain jumps around and I start to feel overwhelmed, my default setting is 'I'm stressed' or 'I'm anxious'. I've learnt, when these feelings emerge, that perhaps the jumpy, jangly sensations are excitement, and I switch my mental vibe accordingly, reminding myself that these are fun things – time-consuming but fun! I try to look at an over-stuffed diary as my kids would, with a 'Yay!' Perception is powerful.

Acknowledge that this too shall pass We all have bad days; some are downright awful. When I have one of those, I take a pause. I break away from what has driven me mad or weakened me. Grab some fresh air, call a good friend, take a shower, or watch a favourite comedy clip on YouTube (Michael McIntyre on parenting will make you feel less ridiculous). And I accept that this is a road bump but that people have it far worse, and I look around to see what I can do to help someone else, something that will help my helplessness by making a positive difference, even if it's just sending a supportive text to a friend who is dealing with something difficult, sharing a friend's new business page on social media or donating to a cousin's fun run. Even small gestures make *everyone* feel better.

Harness your spiralling brain drain As a friend recently said 'I've got 99 problems and 86 of them are completely made up scenarios in my head that I'm stressing about for no logical reason.' Grab a pen and write down your real worries. Dismiss the what-ifs. Reflect on your list when you can feel yourself drifting away from reality.

End a rough day with a bedtime ritual that restores your peace of mind. Ask yourself two questions. 'What am I grateful for today?' You will find something meaningful that might not have occurred to you. 'What am I excited about for tomorrow?' You will look forward to something that will make your mood lift and help you to move on.

Secrets and lies

Perhaps our greatest natural instinct as a parent is the need to protect our children. From the bully in the playground? Yes. From world news that could give them nightmares? Yes. But from things that concern them and they could learn from? Maybe not. Honesty is often the best policy.

Children know when you're not telling them the truth. Their authenticity detectors are way better than ours. Which is why it is often best to share your frazzled brain's worries with them, at a level that is age appropriate, than to leave them in the dark, aware that something is going on and something is being hidden. This will prepare them. Fred Rogers, the iconic American children's writer and entertainer, believed in this policy so much that he even prepared his young fans for his death, leaving a message on his website from him that said, 'Remember that feelings are natural and normal, and that happy times and sad times are part of everyone's life.' Children are more resilient than you think, and as long as information is offered judiciously, in the right context and without malice, a safe version of the truth is better for both of you than building a web of lies.

I know this personally, because I tried to hide my pain from my children until recently. I suffer from migraines, and the difference between my ability to mother when in pain compared to when I'm not makes me look like Dr Jekyll and Mr Hyde. In the middle of one of my 72-hour episodes I find it difficult to laugh, sing, listen or move. My head feels like someone is chipping away at it with an ice pick, while seesawing my jaw with sandpaper. Now my children are at an age where they've learnt to be empathetic, rather than hide my pain or pretend I'm fine, or to allow my snappiness to go unexplained, I share it with them. 'Mummy has a headache, she needs peace and quiet, I'll be back to normal soon, and you have nothing to worry about.' They've responded well to my honesty, enjoying looking after me, rather than worrying about why I had suddenly disappeared, or why I won't let them play music loudly as we drive somewhere.

Closeness when there's a loss

Both my children were also very conscious of the death of my Grandma two years ago. They saw me cry, they looked at photos of her with me, we shared our memories, and we still talk about her and how much we all miss her. They're happy that she's in the stars being serenaded by George Michael and Freddie Mercury. They know it's okay to miss someone so much your heart hurts, and they know it's always okay to share sad feelings. It's the tough physical and emotional challenges we go through as a family that give us a chance to build our fortitude, empathy and self-awareness.

Connecting with your inner child

Motherhood's greatest gift is that we get to experience this beautiful world around us again, the awe and appreciation we sometimes forget to feel as adults reinvigorated by these little people we love unconditionally. Our tired, cynical brains get a reboot, a break from thinking as adults. The restorative effect of embracing our inner child through our offspring is immeasurable: you get to redo the parts of your childhood that have always left you feeling ignored or lesser, it boosts your creativity and encourages you to look at problems in a new way, using your imagination to dream big rather than being weighed down by all the times you've failed in the past. When you allow your brain to live in the moment, at the same level as your child, you worry less, forgetting during that time about unpaid bills, mean bosses or scary deadlines. You can be wrong, and work to make it right without overanalysing yourself and your weaknesses. You can ask questions, or admit that you don't know all the answers, without feeling judged or daft. You can treat your inner child with the same kindness that you treat your real child: you can listen to her, speak lovingly to her, apologise to her and forgive her.

The power of play

We value free play for our children's cognitive, physical and social development, building as it does a child's dexterity, imagination and bonds with family and friends. Play is invaluable to a child's development; in fact, it has been recognised by the United Nations High Commission for Human Rights as a right for every child. But here's a surprise: recent studies have shown it is beneficial to parents, too. George Bernard Shaw wrote, 'We don't stop playing because we grow old; we grow old because we stop playing.' Larking about is worth thinking about because:

- It improves our brain function. Puzzles and board games not only help prevent memory loss, but the social aspect of playing also wards off depression and stress.
- It stimulates our imagination, lending us new tools to fix problems or come up with new ideas. The recognised link

between productivity, innovation and creativity with play time explains the rising number of companies who fill their canteens or lobbies with ping-pong tables and basketball hoops.

- It encourages bonding and strengthens relationships, especially with your own child. Give your child your undivided attention, get down to their level, let them take the lead and teach them things about you that they don't get to see during the hectic school run or while you're trying to get them to bed at a decent time.
- It keeps us youthful, giving us a quick, free-and-easy boost of energy and vitality.
- It reminds us of the importance or cooperation, communication and boundaries. It allows us to confront difficult or awkward situations with good humour and good will.
- It makes motherhood interesting: you and your child can learn and have fun together.

Why did I go upstairs again?

Losing your memory is the biggest mental side effect I've heard my friends complain about since motherhood. A study of 1,000 women published in the *Journal of Clinical and Experimental Neuropsychology* found that pregnancy can reduce a woman's memory function for up to a year after they've given birth. And beyond, I've found. I still forget people's names and people's birthdays, I forget why I'm walking into a room while I'm walking into it! It's easy to understand why we feel this way: as well as the hormonal changes the scientists uncovered, lifestyle factors play a big part: we're not getting enough sleep, our structure is constantly thrown off balance, so we're having to spin a thousand different plates at once, and kid clutter in the home clutters our brains too, as we go from worrying about ourselves to other people, too. And let's not forget the constant interruptions. 'Mama, can I tell you something?' is the current soundtrack to my life. How would I remember someone's name as they are telling me if I have a little person barking at me about how many teeth a shark has at the same time? It is understandably impossible. Plus, we are usually thinking about something else (or ten other things!) on our way to do something, which is why we then can't remember why we went upstairs in the first place.

Easy ways to lighten the mental load

You can show your brain some love by attempting a few things. First, admit to yourself that you now have this problem and write things down. I have a to-do list permanently open on my desk. Not only does it mean I don't forget things, but it gives me a sense of accomplishment when I cross things off. I keep a pen and notepad on my bedside cabinet to note down things that I need to remember for the next day, which helps me go to sleep. I try to do things immediately if at all possible, so that I don't forget to return that email or turn on the oven. I also help myself out by setting specific places in my home where things are kept so that I can't lose them, and I encourage my children to do the same. Shoes live on the same step, bags are hooked up by the front door. And I use my phone as a friendly reminder for appointments or to keep me on schedule.

Internally, some foods are good for the brain: whole grains, fish, nuts, berries and spinach feed your memory. Omega-3, found in salmon, mackerel and other oily fish, walnuts and flaxseeds, is specifically good for memory. And keep drinking, because dehydration can make you mentally as well as physically sluggish.

Anti-social behaviour

According to a 2017 survey, the average Brit checks their social media accounts on their phone 28 times a day. That's once an hour, at least, and 10,000 times a year. We have become Pavlov's dogs to a ping, zombies who often put cyber connections above real ones. When we engage with images and words on social media, strange things happen to our brain – some are positive but most are negative. The good things about keeping up with the world's shenanigans online are the feelings of connection it can give you to friends and family far away. Also, FOMO can be reduced, when you see how your niece's dance recital went or you get to wish your university chum a happy birthday and reminisce about the previous birthday fun you've had together. Social media allows sufficient anonymity that people can share problems or seek out others like them to discuss them with, which will alleviate a sense of loneliness and isolation. Social media can also be used as a motivational tool to live a healthier life. Following someone's journey as they lose weight, give up drinking, or train for a 5k, or sharing your own goals, improves accountability and focus. At a more grass-roots level, social media can help you to learn about things that are happening in your area, and put you in touch with like-minded people.

Mama says: Anne, 37

'I became a mother on 20 January 2006, exactly eight months and six days before Facebook opened enrolment to the general public. I didn't have my own Facebook account for quite a while, but that short-lived period of what I will call "private parenting" was glorious, and I wonder how parenting would be different without this social influence. Online, I was obsessed with what everyone thought about me and my parenting skills, and my ability to make a cake look like a baseball hat. I would never have admitted it, but I thought perfection equalled happiness until I realised that perfect doesn't exist, and now my kids are nine and 12 I no longer feel *obligated* to share their every movement online.'

The social media filter

If we allow social media to replace real-life conversations, interactions or sleep, the effects on our mental health can be damaging. Our brains get overloaded with perfectly filtered photos and other people's happy news, which can have a knock-on effect on our self-esteem. In fact, a study by the University of Copenhagen found that 'Facebook envy' was a real phenomenon, and people who abstained from using Facebook reported feeling more satisfied with their lives. I took it off my phone on New Year's Day and can vouch for the mental uptick.

Social media is also having a detrimental effect on our social skills. For something that connects us, it also disconnects us from meaningful face-to-face quality time. It even stops us from picking up the phone. And if you thought motherhood had had a bad effect on your brain, just read what your phone addiction is doing to it: we're spending so long online rather than being present, filtering photos or styling them to be socially acceptable, that we're not absorbing life as it happens with our own eyes and emotions.

It's also damaging our attention span. When there's easy, quick, constantly changing entertainment at our fingertips, our brains struggle to maintain focus throughout a film or play, or even a half-hour television show. It is making it harder for us to concentrate in all areas of our lives, without our fingers and minds twitching for bright, shiny social news. Most importantly perhaps for mamas is what it does to sleep quality. The light from mobile devices suppresses the sleep hormone melatonin, and feelings of envy or anxiety can overstimulate our brains before bed. Here's how to stop the social media brain drain:

Be conscious of the amount of time you spend on social media per day or per week. Make a note. Four hours? You could have gone to the cinema in that time, read half a great book, cleaned your whole house and had a bubble bath. Instead your brain is just buzzing with what other people have achieved. Being aware of the maths will keep you in check.

Set a strict bedtime routine Try switching off an hour before bed. Go back to using an old-fashioned alarm clock if you're using that as an excuse for keeping your phone next to your bed. Invest in a book light so that you can read.

Practise willpower Be strong. Don't take your phone on family walks. Leave it in the hotel room on holiday. If you use it as a camera – as I do, which I use as my excuse to have it with me at all times – buy a lightweight digital camera and sling that in your bag instead.

If you can't come off everything, choose a platform that can create a hiatus for a while. I recently shut down my Twitter account when I noticed that although Facebook and Instagram gave me more warm, fuzzy feelings than bad ones, Twitter felt like being shouted at in the face by an angry mob. You might worry about feeling disconnected from what's going on, but, honestly, I didn't even remember I'd come off it until I wrote this sentence.

Set up app constraints on your phone. There are programs that chuck you off social media platforms after your pre-set amount of time. Or be strict and set social-media-free times in your house.

We have set one that starts when the kids arrive home after school until their bedtime.

Be part of the solution

One of the greatest skills we can give our kids is to be a problem solver rather than a panicker – and becoming a parent is a great time for you to take a refresher course. Life is tough and mistakes do happen, but you can train yourself as you train your kids to take the lesson from a problem and to move on. The first rule is to allow your child and yourself to take risks. This could lead to failure, so you analyse why and then move on without regret. Don't helicopter your children into a perfect world; let them see that things can be difficult. Talk them through solutions and encourage problem solving with creative play, such as building a house from wooden bricks or making a puppet with only a paper bag and some pens. Talk about issues that you've had that day at work and ask them what they would have done. Get them to help you with DIY, brainstorm ideas to save money from the household budget, talk about the problems your mum and dad had with you growing up and ask them what they would have done differently. Don't be scared to tell your children that the world throws problems at you – and don't forget to tell them about the immense feeling of satisfaction you get from solving them.

Wearing two hats can be hard

All routes of motherhood are complicated and difficult, but perhaps none more so than that of the working mum, who wears two hats, which could both topple off at any second. Firstly, she has to deal with being questioned about whether she is 'enjoying her time off' when she's on maternity leave – an unhelpful statement to working mothers and stay-at-home mothers, because, as anyone who's ever done this knows, there is no harder time in your life. But from then on, the working mother is subject to judgement and evaluation, not least from herself. Do her kids need her around more? Is she giving her professional life enough care and consideration? Is she working because she needs to or because she wants to? Is her partner doing enough, and is he understanding enough? As mothers, we become quite addicted to our children, craving closeness and a symbiotic flow. Before I even understood what motherhood was, I witnessed female bosses crying at their desks, which were surrounded by photos of their cherished children, distraught that they were missing a school play, or foisting their sick child onto a caregiver rather than daring to risk the wrath of their male superiors. They were, quite literally, a mess – and they felt that no one was winning from the working-mother scenario.

My mother, for much of my childhood, had to work. She was on her own, had three jobs, and called on my grandma and aunts for help, and I was trusted to walk home from school and let myself into the house when younger than a child would probably be allowed to today. My mother didn't love it, but she didn't have a choice. She needed the money to run our home. I am lucky and different. I have the choice. I have always worked part-time from home throughout my kids' lives, but I returned to a full-time job when my daughter was one year old, rushing between her day care and my office, and never feeling that I had enough time to do anything. After a year of that, I made the decision to work from home again – which might seem perfect, but I warn you, it means that no one takes you seriously at either. You kind of flit through the middle, an indecisive will-o'-the-wisp: not earning great money, not getting great respect, missing out on adult interaction, and you are often expected to keep an immaculate house and home-cooked meals on the table because 'you're home all day!'.

The decision to return to work

Never does a mama need to engage her Zen mindset more than when she's decided – if she financially has the choice – as to whether she wants to return to work. Think about what is right for you and your child, and then think about what is necessary for your financial situation. Not the extras, or the fripperies and fancies, but the essentials you need in order to have a secure, happy home. Draw a list of needs and wants, and how much it would cost. Then add the cost of childcare, which often throws things off balance. Be realistic about how much family members are prepared to help you out, and consider the emotional costs of asking them. Some grandparents are too tired to take on the care of young children – they raised their own and want to enjoy the grandkids on a more sporadic basis. This is not selfish; this is honest and fair.

Don't rose-tint being at home with your children, though. Your kid boss can be more unreasonable than your real boss and expect you to work longer hours. Don't feel pushed into quitting your job by people from a different generation with different values, or by stay-at-home mum friends who may be tickled with the *Schadenfreude* brush rather than your best interests. Staying at home is not easier. There will be no lunch breaks, or coffee shop meetings, or gossip in the loos. You might be able to wear pyjamas for longer, but is that really a perk?

The delicate balance

Discuss returning to work with your partner, too. This is not a decision to be made in your head alone. You are a team. How will the balance shift between household and financial responsibilities if you decide to stay at home rather than going out to work? And if you decide to go back to work after a period at home, your partner has to realise that his life will not stay the same either: they'll have to pick up more slack around the house and regarding childcare.

You also need to think, on one level, about your future as separate from the kids' future. What will staying at home do for your long-term career plans? Is a break acceptable? Could you work part-time? Could you take on freelance projects that would keep your name alive in the industry, or keep you up to date with your colleagues and cohort?

Ultimately, you should know that well-adjusted healthy children, both sons and daughters are raised by stay-at-home mums *and* working mums. Children just respond well to happy mums, so look carefully into what would bring you the most joy, and then look realistically at how this can work for all your family. Also, you should note that nothing is set in stone. After a year as a working mother in a newsroom, I shifted back to working part-time from home, and I'm sure the children didn't even notice. Nothing is forever. Adapt to your needs and their ages. And focus on streamlining your lives to be the most efficiently pleasing for you all.

Passed-on paranoia

Before I became a mother, I experienced soul-crushing bouts of self-doubt and paranoia. Did my boss hate me? Why did my old friend seem to prefer her new friend over me? Why did I not make the guest list for that girl's weekend away? I was often ready to feel lesser, unwanted, singled out and unlovable, focusing on the relationships that I didn't have rather than the amazing ones that I did and nurturing those. In my late twenties a wise woman said to me plainly, 'Not everyone will love you, so concentrate on loving the ones who do, even better.' This gave me such a positive brain-switch! Nurture the love you have found, rather than worrying about the love you haven't. I was successful at this until my son started school, and I pushed my deep-seated fears on to him. Why was he excluded from that fifth birthday party? Why didn't he have a play date every weekend like some kids? My inner child – the one who was bullied and left out – came out in a sad combination of broken kid and ferocious mama bear. If I could have wrapped William in cotton wool and given him the sun and the moon, I would have done so. Instead, I revisited my wise friend's words and got a fresh perspective on my brain's issues around friendship. I asked myself these questions:

- Does my son seem bothered by any of this, or is this my stuff? For my son, only 1 per cent of the time.
- Am I making an effort to build relationships, or hiding in my shell expecting things to come to me? (I was expecting others to make the effort first, worried about being rebuffed.)
- Is he really being left out, or am I glossing over all the good stuff to focus on the bad? (I was giving more energy to the one party he was excluded from than the three he went to.)
- Why am I questioning if my son is good enough to join their gang, when my question should be 'Are they good enough for my son?' (Sometimes a kid is a bully, and my job as a parent is to teach my child to be resilient and to recognise the beauty in true friends.)

Mama says: Laura, 35

'I used to find myself yelling at my kids a lot. When we were running late and they dragged their feet, when they refused to clean up, or when they would fight, my typical response would be to yell at them. Afterwards, I would vow to myself to be a better mother and pray for guidance, but it wouldn't be long before I found myself yelling at them once more. Over the past couple of months that has changed. I have become a much calmer, more loving mother. The reason for this is as simple as it is surprising: as the outside world becomes more divided and tough, I feel an urge to make their home life loving and gentle. When my kids are running late for school now, I no longer yell at them to get ready. I urge them kindly and help them as needed. When they refuse to clean up a mess, I bribe them with treats or threaten to take away a privilege, but I don't yell. When they fight, I talk to them about treating others with kindness and put them in time-out if necessary, but I don't yell.'

The emotion commotion

One change that no one ever warns you about is the lack of control you will now have over your tear ducts. This only gets worse. After William was born I discovered that I now cry at Christmas adverts and romantic films, I cry when I see a beautiful flower, receive a thoughtful message from a friend, or hear a love song that reminds me of my youth. I've had to ban The Smiths. I even sob publicly at children's concerts that – and here's the crying kicker – don't even have my children in them. I cry when anyone's child does something brave or beautiful. I don't believe mothers are more empathetic and sympathetic than non-mothers (some of my kindest, most considerate friends are not mothers), I just believe that motherhood loosens your guard a little, sends your hormones a bit loopy, and makes you wear your heart on your sleeve a little more. Embrace it. What the world needs now is love, sweet love.

Intellectual self-care

'Since I had a kid, all I talk about is poo!' I hear this all the time. Even when women can manage a conversation among the million distractions and divergences that motherhood throws at us, the subject matter can be rather dull or gruesome. Our brains are not slowing down, but our focus has narrowed, sometimes to our own detriment, and we need to look after our brains as much as our bodies if we want to feel useful, valued and vital. And do keep a check on your baby talk when you're with non-parents who will find vaccine discussions extremely tedious. Look after your mind and keep conversation interesting with a few of these pastimes:

- Join your local library and spend a few minutes every month choosing a book.
- Listen to a radio programme or podcast that keeps you up to date with world news.
- Watch documentaries that stimulate your brain rather than watching bubblegum soaps.
- Visit art galleries and museums with a friend, or during baby's nap time when they can be pushed around in a buggy.
- Ask for a subscription to a newspaper or specialist magazine as a birthday gift.
- Play games that challenge your brain such as chess, draughts, Articulate!, and so on.
- Keep a journal or sketchbook by your bed to note creative thoughts.
- Volunteer for a local charity to meet new and different types of people.

Your PG rating

Read these Ps and Gs then write down and plan your family's priorities going forward.

The Ps:

Purpose To stay sane during the turbulence of constant family change.

Perspective This is a tough time mentally as well as physically. Appreciate that.

Presence I'll learn from today and move on tomorrow.

The Gs:

Gratitude My mind is busy because my life is so full.

Goals I'll stop worrying about the things that I cannot change and focus on improving the things that I can.

Going for it Marry your head and heart, and make decisions from your gut.

TAKE A DEEP BREATH, MAMA

Flip your brain switch to an attitude of gratitude and a mindset of mindfulness. You cannot live in reaction to your child, or your boss, or your Instagram page. You are living as a result of you doing the best job you can do, today, in your way, nothing more and nothing less. You're surviving, and you're thriving – even if you don't feel like it in this moment. You should be proud.

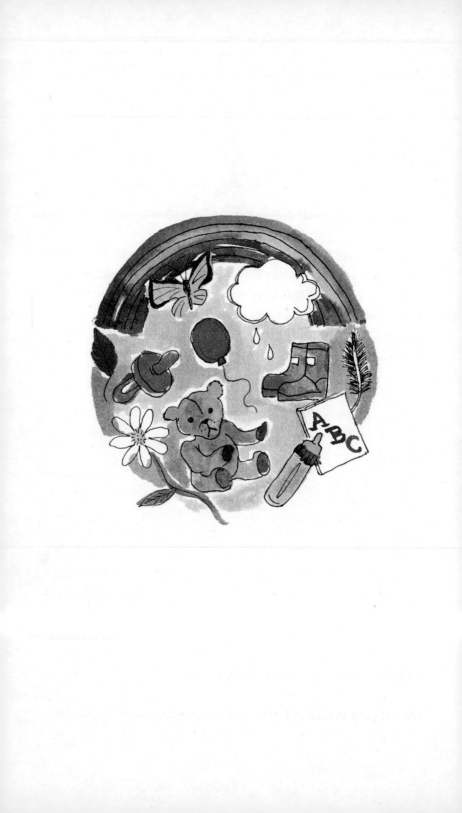

6

Create a Serene Home

'If they would all sleep all the time she wouldn't mind being their mother'

Kate Atkinson, Case Histories

Home is where we go to rest, recuperate and rejuvenate from the hollering of the outside world. Well, it should be, but often the detritus of family life makes this impossible and our home becomes a dumping ground for clutter and complaints, making it as crazy as school or the office. We can make it a safe space, though, a place where we can let off steam and be ourselves, which is a must for parents and children alike, physically and mentally.

Jane Austen wrote that 'there is nothing like staying home for real comfort' and we can create a cocoon from the world's dramas and disruptions with a little thought and care.

Use all your senses to feather your nest. Spray mood-enhancing essential oils and light naturally scented candles to fill your home with an aroma that uplifts (try grapefruit, rosemary, juniper) or relaxes (try sandalwood, chamomile, lavender). Paint your bedrooms in pastels and pale shades to soothe you to sleep, and lift the spirits in family rooms with energising yellow and orange. Keep windows and windowsills clear and clean to allow natural light to flood your house with warmth, and bring nature indoors with fresh flowers and potted plants. If you want background noise, turn off the television and play music instead.

Welcome yourself home with mottos that mean something. Choose positive, life-affirming phrases to frame around the house, reminding you of family goals and the family unit. We have a sign that says 'Be nice or leave' by our front door to remind everyone who enters that this is a haven of kindness.

Japanese organising guru, Marie Kondo, tells us that peace of mind comes with a decluttered home, so look at every item in your house, and if you don't use it or love it, take it to a charity shop or recycle it. If anything is broken and unfixable, bin it. Calm your mind and make things easier to find in a hurry by creating open spaces.

Fill your home with things that make you smile – heirlooms that remind you of happy stories and lovely people from your past, framed photos of family holidays, sea shells from beach days and books that help you escape. Our fridge is covered with the kids' artwork, pinned up with magnets given to us by friends, a cosy reminder of things important to us.

Get in the Zen zone and give each space in your home a unique purpose that reflects your family values and goals. Ban electronic devices from bedrooms, and stack books next to your pillow instead. Turn a corner of your living room into a crafts centre, placing colourful felt pens, pencils and crayons in pretty Kilner jars as part of the room's decor. Make board games easily accessible next to the television, and you'll be more persuaded to play them than if they're hidden at the back of a dusty cupboard. Put any instruments you play out on display, rather than in a case, forgotten about in a bedroom. Get the children involved in decorating their bedrooms, so that they reflect their personalities and interests and they feel invested in keeping them tidy, using them for quiet time, or hosting play dates in them.

Mama says: Natasha, 40

'I wouldn't say that I fully subscribe to the "tiger mum" method, but somehow over time our life has got pretty hectic. My husband and I both work full-time, but if our children want to do extra-curricular activities, our philosophy is that if we can make the logistics work, we will say yes. We regularly check in, and if they're still having fun, we keep juggling. I think, like all kids, they still like some level of consistency and comfort that we attempt to build into an ever-changing daily schedule. On Sundays, we will look at the calendar for the week and try our best to forecast when we will (or will not) be able to have family time in the evening. During family dinner, we talk about our "favourite parts of the day". They get excited about sharing, and it provides a launching point for a story that gives more detail on the day. Every evening I'm home, I sing "Twinkle Twinkle" at bedtime. I have been doing this since Beth was born, and it is amazing how this short song puts punctuation into the end of our day.'

We will chill!

Switching off and regrouping as a family is a priority in this busy world. It re-bonds us and reconnects us to values, goals and priorities, giving our hectic lives some order and continuity. When our children are tiny, we can't help but hibernate and hide away, but as they grow up and away from the tight-knit family unit, parents have to work a bit harder to maintain closeness. Your kids will thank you for it when they get older and look back on their childhood, and you'll treasure the memories, too. When a grandmother said to me during my frazzled first weeks of motherhood, 'The days are long but the years are short', I wanted to slap her. Now, as mine approach the pre-teen era of natural distancing and closer friendships, I wish I could shake her by the hand for the warning. Here are some very easy, free pastimes to try at home:

A Friday night film night is something most families love. It gives maximum relaxing results with minimum effort – needed after a busy week. Use Google to make lists of films about a theme (Christmas, New York, cats, bravery, for example), pop some corn and snuggle under a double duvet. You could also make your own films: draw a cartoon-style storyboard, choose who will play which character and get creative.

Family discos shake off the day's gripes. Get a mirror ball or fairy lights going, pull on something sparkly from your wardrobe, and introduce your children to the songs you loved as a child, then let them play you songs their friends have been loving (do not dismiss their taste; remember you hated it when your parents didn't understand the talent of Bros or Britney Spears). Work out some group dance routines.

Make a camp – indoors or outside – and tell ghost stories by lamplight. Blanket forts are fun, or erect a tent if you have one. Pack treats and hot chocolate. Bring books about nature and wildlife to read aloud, and discuss how animals stay warm at night, imagine their family life, where they live etc. We have just read *Fantastic Mr Fox* by Roald Dahl, which was perfect for this.

Open a restaurant one evening: choose a theme, don aprons, and draw up menus. The kids can help you prepare and cook, and then act as waiters once you're ready to sit down. If a meal is too much, baking biscuits or decorating a pizza is fun and low-drama.

Have a night at the theatre – in your living room. Play charades, dress up in funny costumes, host a show-and-tell, get out the karaoke machine, or take it in turns to tell jokes. Brush up on your Shakespeare with some child-friendly retelling of his classics.

Electric youth

Undoubtedly, we all rely on media to help us escape from the real world at home these days, but we need to consume a healthy diet of it rather than gorge gormlessly if we want to set a good example to our offspring. You have to walk the walk not just talk the talk, and use your devices in the same way that you want your kids to use theirs (not at bedtime, not at meal times, not in the park). Then, as a family, make good decisions and look for quality games, films and shows that are age appropriate for all. Play, watch and listen together, and use the topics to discuss real-world things, encouraging everyone's passions (I have watched more documentaries about the Titanic, NASA and Henry VIII than I would perhaps have liked, but the excitement of my husband and son got me through it), but keep an eye on the clock. Don't allow screen time to replace other family bonding activities like those listed above or to eat up hours to the detriment of fresh air, exercise and sleep.

Sibling rivalry

We all want to feel special, so I've worked hard to create special time for each of my children alone, away from their sibling. Most nights, my son gets to sneak in an episode of *Fawlty Towers* or *Upstart Crow* with me and his dad after we've settled his younger sister – and he tells me that this is his favourite time of the day. As I pull Matilda's door shut, he appears, winks at me, and whispers, 'This is our time!' and we tiptoe downstairs. He plays football in the park with his dad while I take his sister to the book shop, and before our holidays Matilda and I go and get a pedicure in a massage chair and flick through travel magazines looking for ideas. Space from their sibling gives each child time to talk about things that are bothering them – and to be sure that they have their parent's undivided attention. Please, please, put your phone away during this time.

Non-warring siblings are a crucial part of creating a serene home. Mine have gone from being very thoughtful and sweet to each other to being hyper-competitive in the last few years. A mama can often fall into the trap of assuming her children are (a) similar; and (b) friends, because they share the same *nurture* and *nature*. But they all pop out as their own beings, and forcing them to be together all the time, doing the same things and sharing everything can make them feel stifled. For your peace of mind – and a peaceful atmosphere in your home – you should avoid comparing them to each other all the time, and keep praise equal. Set ground rules on the behaviour you find unacceptable and encourage and reward kind behaviour. Listen to your children when they have problems, but try not to get drawn into every little argument they have with each other. Give them a role to play, a clear position in the family: the older child can learn responsibility from teaching his younger sibling about life, and get a confidence boost from being looked up to as he teaches, while the younger sibling can get a jumpstart on facts and figures from their older sibling that will give them playground kudos with their peers and become more self-sufficient. Treat them – and your partner – in the way in which you would like them to treat their sibling: with love, affection and generosity.

An appetite for love

Eating together as a family can be difficult, but carving out time to dine en masse at least a couple of times a week will benefit you all. It doesn't have to be dinner, if working keeps you too late to prepare a meal. Make your life work for Saturday brunch, or afternoon tea on Sundays. You'll have time to sit and talk about your days, your children will get the chance to experiment with new, healthy foods not served up during their usual course of the day, and you'll instil in them a love for food and conversation that will take them through life. Without you having to tell them, your kids will see you choose water over fizzy drinks, and enjoying your vegetables, and they will be subconsciously swayed in your direction. Enlist the whole family to get teatime team spirit: one person can set the table, another can cook, one can serve, and you can clean up together. Family dining builds a sense of security and belonging, according to a study of teenagers completed by Columbia University, and reduces stress and tension for all family members, as reported by researchers at Brigham Young University.

Farewell, Sleeping Beauty

Perhaps the single most important thing we all *hope* to do at home is get a good night's sleep. Motherhood tends to change all that.

Yes, nowhere does becoming a mum hit harder than between the hours of 7pm and 7am, those decadent hours when as a pre-mama you could choose between rest and relaxation or fun and frolics. A friend recently sent me a great card with a quote on it: 'The joys of motherhood are never truly appreciated until the children are asleep in bed.' How true! I remember longing for the moment when my baby and toddler children were clean, fed and sleepy and we could lay them down in their bedrooms for a 12-hour respite (12 hours depending on their mood, teeth, ability to play fair to their harangued parents, and so on). But the strangest things would happen! As soon as they were down, I'd miss them. I'd tell my husband about all the cute little things they'd done that day, all the new accomplishments and friends. Sometimes, when we should have been sleeping ourselves, we – the soppy pair – would even watch videos of them, or flick through photo collections, and marvel at what wonderful children we had. Indeed, when they're sleeping, children *are* perfect. My five-year-old still rarely sleeps through the night, and my body and mind only get to rest in a semi-comatose state awaiting her yell for water, a cuddle or a tarantula check (she's convinced they live in her wardrobe). Being able to sleep is probably the thing I miss most from my pre-child days, but I've fallen into a level of acceptance and survival. Firstly, it's amazing how productive you can be with little sleep, and it's astonishing what a combination of coffee, concealer, chewing mint gum and a blast of fresh air and sunlight can do for a withered soul.

Nightmare on Elmo Street

My mother tried to warn me. 'You'll never sleep again!' she said when I was moaning in my eighth month of pregnancy with William about my flattened bladder and constant night-time trips to the loo. One night, I was so frequent, I decided to take a book in with me and just sit out the fifteen-minute respites from weeing on the toilet instead of waddling back to bed and attempting to get comfy. 'Once the baby comes, he'll keep you up all night. And then he'll settle into a routine, and eventually start sleeping through the night, but you'll imagine you hear crying, or have bad dreams about dropping him or leaving him in the supermarket. And your bladder will be destroyed in childbirth and you'll still need to do the frequent trips to the loo.' Unperturbed by her negativity, I replied that I'm sure by the time he was a playing, energetic toddler, we'd both be too exhausted to stay awake for real reasons like teething pain, or imaginary ones. 'Oh darling, you're so naive,' she countered. 'I'm trying to prepare you! You will *never* sleep soundly again. When you and your brothers were in primary school, I couldn't sleep because I was so worried you couldn't keep up in class. At high school, I sat up all night worried that you were being bullied – then I worried that you wouldn't pass your driving test, and then I worried when you did. At university, I worried about you taking drugs. In your twenties, I watched as you got your hearts broken. And even now that you are in your forties, I still worry and lose sleep over you. I worry about your own journey to motherhood. Your brothers are grown men, but I worry about them being happy in their careers and paying their mortgages.' A long, long life of dark circles suddenly appeared before me. 'This is a mother's lot,' she confirmed. 'You will never, ever sleep like a baby after you've had your own baby.' As I started banging my head on the kitchen table, she quickly added something encouraging. 'It's all worth it! I wouldn't change any of it or any of you for the world!' She was right.

Mama says: Francesca, 29

'Cake is the answer. Always cake. One of my personal triumphs of motherhood is getting over my previous fear of calories and embracing the delicious pep-me-up qualities of sugary lemon drizzle cake or a Victoria sponge. The less sleep eight-month-old Marie gives me, the more slices I'm allowed to consume. I think women can be too tough on themselves. Lack of sleep is a form of internationally recognised torture. So, don't get sucked into the pressure of being flawless on three hours of kip – enjoy sweet stuff, mainline coffee, overshare with your mates. All is fair in the battle of you and your bed.'

Shower survival on zero sleep

Yes, yes – people will tell you the best way to avert crushing exhaustion is to get to the gym and do a workout. They are right of course, and on the occasions I did do it when I had tiny ones at home I felt the benefit. But this is difficult when you have a baby/child strapped to you all day, or you're struggling to spend enough quality time with your offspring outside your working week as it is. In my early mama days, the quickest, easiest method for elevating tiredness was to take a ten-minute shower. Now, grabbing ten minutes to yourself can seem like a challenge – especially in the beginning – but it can be done. I would place my baby just outside the open bathroom door in a vibrating chair. I could see and hear him, he could see and hear me, and this ten-minute rejuvenation potion was possible:

1. Turn the water from warmer to cooler to jolt some life into your body.

2. Do some bends and stretches. Let's call it hydro-yoga.

3. Purchase a shower gel with one of the following ingredients to instantly pep up your brain: lemon, orange, peppermint, sage, vanilla or coconut.

4. Exfoliate all your body if you can, or just your face if you don't have much time. You'll feel super-clean and new. Use one with salt in it for a really tough scrub. Invest in a body brush or glove.

5. Treat yourself to a luxurious shampoo and conditioner. Even if you don't get the time to blow-dry your hair (although, tip alert: most babies feel soothed by the sound of a hairdryer, as it mimics the sounds they heard in the womb), you'll feel better just having clean, smooth hair.

To nap, perchance to dream

I heard the phrase 'sleep while the baby's sleeping' more than any other during my first few months of motherhood. This seems to be a lifesaver for lots of women, so if you can do it, do it. Don't procrastinate with Twitter. Get your head down the minute your little one does. And, for God's sake, put that duster down! Housework can wait. Nap.

If, like me, you found daytime napping impossible, at least take the opportunity to rest. Catch up with your favourite, wonderfully mind-numbing reality show or take a relatively long soak in the bath with a magazine (15 minutes – wahoo!). On a nice day, sit out in the garden and get some sun on your skin and some fresh air in your lungs (both can do wonders). Whatever you do, don't miss your chance to take it easy. The world can wait.

Mama says: Hannah, 30

'Accept what you cannot change. My two-year-old boy is terrified of sleeping alone and is still in our bed. It's not what we want by any means, but we have accepted that that's who he is. Sleep training just never worked for him. The funny thing is my six-foot-five-inch husband was the same as a toddler, and he grew up to be a bodyguard! Find quiet and solitude where you can. Roll with the sleeplessness. When my baby was little, instead of going back to sleep when he woke me up I would stay awake and watch television with pleasure in the middle of the night. It was the only time to be still and quiet. It made me tired during the day, but I needed the mental break of me time to be awake but not working or taking care of a child.'

Give yourself the best opportunity for sleep

Use light to your advantage Try to stick to a regular sleep pattern if you can, and get lots of bright sunlight during the day (leave the house!) and minimise bright lights at night. Don't watch television or work on a computer the half hour before you want to sleep. Invest in blackout curtains – for your room and the nursery.

Sip serenity My restorative yoga instructor swears by a soothing cup of golden milk (warm milk spiced with nutmeg, cinnamon, turmeric and ginger) before bedtime. Ovaltine will do the trick, too. But cut down on heavy meals, alcohol and caffeine – and avoid drinking too much liquid in the hour before bedtime so that you're not on the loo all night.

Find your optimum relaxation temperature A bath before bed will bring on the zzzzzs. A drop in body temperature at night is one of the classic signals for the body to start producing melatonin, the hormone that induces sleep. Speed up the downward shift by heating yourself up artificially with a warm soak. Get out of a bath, cool yourself down for a while, then slip into bed. Keep your room cool (18ºC is perfect). Adjust your bedding for the season.

If you're too tired to read, listen to books on tape or close your eyes and try deep breathing, meditating and visualisation. A meditation teacher taught me that breathing in and out through your nostrils – in for four seconds, hold for four seconds, out for eight seconds – has a naturally sedating effect.

Stop fearing the next day, because once you stop anxiously awaiting sleep, or fearing how you'll be with a lack of it in the morning, you'll drift off easier. Tell yourself you'll survive whatever, because you have before. You got this.

Let go of the lie-in dream

The dream of a lie-in could be lying dormant for a few years, mama, so you must use those early mornings to do other restorative acts, not seething in a storm of frustration and cereal. I would get so irritated when my kids appeared like clockwork at 6am every weekend, especially after a week of having to shake them out of bed at 7am on school days. Every Saturday I'd hope for a bit more sleep, and scowl like The Grinch at the sound of their little footsteps rather than greeting them with glee and a 'good morning'. I got over myself by just being honest. It wasn't going to happen. Even when they had a late night, they'd be up early. I refocused my brain to take their early wake-up call calmly. I get up, resembling a slightly dishevelled zombie, I won't lie, and I head down to make their breakfast and get them situated with a project or – I'm not perfect – a Disney film. Then I foresee the next hour's drama and plan accordingly (put toothpaste on their toothbrush, refill water bottles, give them the television remote, lay out the requested leisurewear), then I make a coffee and go back to bed. I might not be asleep, but I still get to rest. When they're a bit older, I've been told you can move into evening prep to buy time: either teach them how to make their own breakfast (and your coffee, mama, make them useful!) or lay out what you can, and teach them how to use Netflix.

Bye-bye bedtime routine

The greatest skill of a serene-ish parent is to go with the flow and let things drift at their natural pace, engaging the Zen talent for trusting your instincts, appreciating your own need for downtime and dropping any illusions of perfection. You are not a machine and your lives are not uniform and unflappable. When the day runs away from you, dinner can be simple, quick or delivered. The nutritionally dubious can be amped up with a side of carrots and apple slices so that you can hold the serving of mum guilt or mum fear. Bath time can be abandoned; in fact, I was married to a nightly dip for my kids (I could trap them in one place for half an hour, which was handy after a long day) until their paediatrician pointed out that kids don't need to be squeaky clean, and in fact baths should be skipped for half the week. If your kids are half asleep, bedding down in their undies is fine, and they're not going to need wooden teeth if they miss the occasional teeth cleaning. Don't drag things out when you're all exhausted and the biggest boost to your own serenity will be shutting up the mama shop for the night and heading to bed yourself.

Just say no

Overscheduling is a modern menace. Our FOMO is clouding our better judgement and making us say yes to things we know won't make us happy. In fact, trying to cram in too much, even seemingly fun things, can add to our exhaustion. Stop saying yes blindly to every invitation. Let discernment be your friend. If you have to allot time for an early night in your diary, write it in – in ink. Do the same with family-only nights, school project nights, hair-wash nights. Pin a calendar up in the kitchen so that you all know what is happening, and sync up your electronic calendar with your partner's so that you're not ships that pass in the night. You've made your home a haven; you need time to enjoy it – together. Stop accepting invitations, and accept what your family *really* needs. Prioritise what is important to your gang. Cancel anything that doesn't add to your goals, educate or excite you. Don't be afraid to share your priorities. If you clearly state that you're not into ballet, cooking classes or opera, you'll stop having to feel guilty about saying no to those things again and again when friends ask you. When you do get invited to things, don't feel under pressure to say yes right away – check your diary and check in with yourself. Do you want to do it? Do your children? Always respond, though. Not giving an answer within a reasonable amount of time is pure bad manners. Don't overload your itinerary. If you'd quite like to do it, make sure you're not taking on too much. You don't want to pack so much in that you spend the whole day worrying about traffic, tiredness and being late rather than enjoying one or two events wholeheartedly. *Squeezing* in fun is not an option. Don't *squeeze* in anything.

Born free

Just as important as saying no to doing too much outside the home is saying yes to free time in the home. Going out and pursuing interests is important but overscheduling your children with hobbies and interests *of yours* or activities you feel they *should* be doing could make them anxious and stressed, and leave you feeling like a taxi driver with holes in your pockets. Free time is crucial for imaginative play – to build creativity and independence – and sporadic play dates in the house or in the back garden allows them to build relationships with their peers outside an instructor's watchful gaze. By chilling out at home you'll also be modelling a behaviour to them that you don't have to be active, rushed and busy all the time, that there is happiness to be found in solitude, silence and making your own entertainment; these are important skills for their mental health as they grow up.

The story of us

In her charming manual on the power of reading to children, *The Enchanted Hour*, book critic, Meghan Cox Gurdon, makes a case for bringing story time back into the home as a regular part of the family routine. 'Reading storybooks turns out to be an extraordinarily efficient and productive way to cause messages to zing from one part of the brain to another, creating and reinforcing those important neural connections.' The American Academy of Pediatrics recently advised its doctors to recommend that parents read aloud to their children, as it 'strengthens parent-child relationships ... builds language, literary, and social-emotional skills that last a lifetime.' Story time develops our imagination, creativity and connections with each other – and it is a much healthier way to unwind from the day than staring at an LED-lit screen. 'If reading aloud were a pill,' writes Cox Gurdon, 'every child in the country would get a prescription.' Use reading aloud as a way to unwind and cuddle up as a family unit as often as possible.

Kindness on every page

Ten books to encourage empathy in your avid readers:

Have You Filled a Bucket Today? A Guide to Daily Happiness for Young Children by Carol McCloud and Katherine Martin

A Sick Day for Amos McGee by Philip C. Stead and Erin E. Stead

Those Shoes by Maribeth Boelts

The Invisible Boy by Trudy Ludwig

Stella's Starliner by Rosemary Wells

Wolf in the Snow by Matthew Cordell

I Walk with Vanessa: A Story About a Simple Act of Kindness by Kerascoët

The Lord of The Rings by J.R.R. Tolkein

To Kill a Mockingbird by Harper Lee

Harry Potter and the Philosopher's Stone by J. K. Rowling

Your PG rating

Note, score and plan your family's priorities using the key words below to set your ambitions going forward.

The Ps:

Purpose To build and maintain a serene home.

Perspective The world can be tough, our home will be safe and warm.

Presence Stepping through the front door should be a comfort to us all.

The Gs:

Gratitude Be thankful for a roof over your head, a place to protect and nurture family.

Goals To adapt the space you have for maximum enjoyment and relaxation.

Going for it Bring in healthier work–life balance measures today.

TAKE A DEEP BREATH, MAMA

Home is a safe space for you and your children to make mistakes, take second chances and have the opportunity to apologise, knowing that you are shielded from the world outside. Home is a perfect place for you and your children to turn the mundane into something magical, and make memories to last a lifetime. Home is where your heart lives.

7

Find Your Tribe

'Think where man's glory most begins and ends, and say my
glory was I had such friends.'

William Butler Yeats

The benefits of finding a group of like-minded, kind-hearted
humans to nestle yourself among cannot be overestimated. I am
often floored by the generosity and thoughtfulness that comes my
way from the women I have gathered around me, the female force
who form a protective barrier between me and the harshness and
monotony that can come as a side dish to motherhood, my cheerleaders and reality checks combined. Some of these connections
are the most important of my life, uncomplicated by attraction,
gender differences or familial overfamiliarity. If asked what my
greatest skill is, I would say it is my ability to locate wonderful
women and persuade them to be my friend. But in this era of
24/7 parenting, social media self-obsession and a focus on sex
lives, platonic friendships often fall under the radar – a great mistake! Aside from the empty hours great mates can fill in a week,

replacing loneliness and unrest with hilarity, camaraderie and empathy, they boost mental and physical well-being, too.

Recent studies have shown how peer pressure can be a good thing, and that surrounding ourselves with inspirational friends can remind us to exercise, take supplements, check our worrying symptoms at the doctor's and eat better. Good friends also give us a sense of purpose and belonging, which gives us another motivational boost to look after ourselves.

There is truth in the old wives' tale that a problem shared is a problem halved. In her book *How Mothers Love: And How Relationships Are Born*, psychotherapist Naomi Stadlen highlights the comfort and reassurance mothers find together when their stories are shared in a collective whole. 'Listening to one another, mothers can hear each of them is fallible,' she writes about her time studying mothers for her work.

> They suddenly realise they have put the mothering benchmark up way too high. In a group, the harsh judgements a mother may give herself when she is on her own at home are softened. The unsolved questions are still there. But the sense of failure she felt at home has changed.

Science backs up Stadlen's observations. An essay published by the Mayo Clinic explains how good friends improve self-confidence and self-worth and help get you through a trauma such as divorce, illness or the death of a loved one.

When life gets busy or fraught, time with friends is often the first thing to be discarded, these relationships are put on the back burner while other things take precedent. Perhaps we do this because we know we can – our peers are the ones who understand the life stage we're in, after all – but as a wealth of information linking loneliness and depression emerges, so should our focus on maintaining meaningful connections. Friends could save your life – literally. A study published in the journal *PLOS Medicine* highlights how social isolation can be as bad for your health as smoking or obesity. When we feel supported, another study shows, our blood pressure lowers, we have a stronger immune system and we display better hormone function.

An anti-social agenda

We shouldn't underestimate the value of engaging with friends face-to-face, or hearing their voices. Although social media can give us the sense of being connected, liked and engaged – and this is true to an extent, and it does have its benefits – it cannot replace the familiarity and closeness of real contact. A 2016 study of 3,300 Britons by researchers at the University of Oxford highlighted how even though the average respondents had 155 Facebook 'friends', the number of people they felt would be there for them in a time of distress was just four, emphasising how although these social-media relationships are fun and convenient, they might not replace the need for a deeper, truer connection. It can be hard and intimidating, but pick up the phone rather than just looking at it. Engage in face-to-face conversations, not just online debates.

Hug it out

The benefits of a hug from someone you love – only available in person, not via a screen – are innumerable. Physical contact with a friend, studies show, reduces stress by showing support. It doesn't matter if you're the hugger or the huggee, it's good for everyone involved. Oxytocin is called the 'cuddle hormone' for good reason, as the chemical is released when we hug, touch or sit close to someone we love, be it a partner, a child or a friend, reducing the amount of the stress hormone norepinephrine rushing around our bodies. In a study of 400 people, those with a greater support system and physical contact were less likely to get sick, and those who still got sick experienced less severe symptoms than those with few or no loved ones around them. Hugs boost your heart, lowering blood pressure and heart rate. Touch reduces anxiety in people with low self-esteem, and various forms of touch (from hugging to massage) can reduce pain. Perhaps, most importantly and obviously, getting a hug from a friend is a quick-and-easy way to communicate support and affection, to comfort both the giver and the receiver, non-transferable in even the wittiest, loveliest email or Instagram post. Stop this touch-deprived society we're living in! See your friends and hug them – your brains and bodies will both benefit. Don't forget to cuddle your kids, too, however annoying you're finding them in a particular moment. Five to ten hugs a day should be a government health suggestion alongside the five to ten fruit and vegetables a day recommendation.

Lonely hearts ad: friends required

Motherhood, whatever stage your child is at, can be confusing and lonely, so good friends who understand your life and its difficulties are crucial. But how do you make new friends as an adult? When you're young it's easy, right? You're forced into groups at school, university and dance class, and those connections click and stick. Yes, you can bond with people at work, but often those relationships stay career-focused and fizzle out when one of you leaves the job. What you need as a mama is a group of parents who get your gripes and will listen to them without thinking you dull, who keep the same limited hours you keep, and who don't mind your conversations being interrupted a million times or being deafened in one ear as you bark like a fishwife at your children over their heads. Mama friendships have their challenges (will your children get on? Will your partners? Will your parenting philosophies fit?) but they are worth pursuing, so, get friend-dating:

Sign up for support Before baby even arrives, put your name down for antenatal classes in your community, or log in to helpful online groups, and follow lively and relevant blogs. Not only will this give you information about what to expect, but it will also get you communicating with people at exactly the same life and parenting stages as your own.

Volunteer Join an activity or club with a wide range of people with whom you might have a clear connection.

Relight old friendships Reconnect with people from your past who you've always admired and thought of fondly but life took you in different directions. Take the initiative, especially if you discover that they're parents now, too.

Dare to befriend If you meet someone at a social gathering you connect with, go out on a limb and tell them how much you enjoyed meeting them, and ask if they'd like to see you again. It's kind of like asking for a date, but without the need to worry about matching underwear.

Extend and accept invitations Give it a trial, for a month. Be more out in the world, and let more people into yours.

Get fit Find a friend at one of the mum with stroller fitness classes, or by joining a local gym that offers free childcare so that you can get a dance class in with like-minded mothers while your children are safe nearby.

Get out into your community Walk the dog or your kids, and start running local errands on foot. Engage with your neighbours and local shopkeepers to find out about other parents in the area, strike up a conversation with people at the kids' classes in the library.

Chase your passions rather than people. They might help you to make longer lasting connections. Think back over your pre-kid life and the hobbies you loved, and pick them up again. This will boost your self-esteem, which will make it feel easier to chat and charm new people – and they'll be people who can bring your old and new interests together. Finding a mama with the same pastime passion will feel like a double win.

Mama says: Eleanor, 43

'I cannot recommend doing an NCT class more. On a gorgeous bank holiday weekend in May, hubby and I spent both days in a musty-smelling scout hut learning about labour, feeding, PND, PNP, life after birth and everything in between. It was the best £150 I've ever spent! These six ladies (and their partners) have now been beside me for over seven years. We set up our own Facebook group for sanity during those night feeds, drank copious amounts of lukewarm hot drinks together, asked for and gave advice, and we have been each other's rock in good and bad times. I know not everyone will be as lucky as I was, and I am grateful every day for these women.'

Old friends are gold friends, kids or not!

Making space and time for your oldest friends who are not parents when you become a mother is crucial for your short- and long-term sanity. No one knows you better, can bring a smile to your face, or can cut straight to the chase with sound advice like someone who has seen you grow up, knows your family history and handles your quirks. Equally, you need to be there for them, too. You might have gone through a massive change, and motherhood is a huge one, but other changes will feel just as big to them: a new relationship, a difficult job, a move to a new city. Bear in mind that we all face our own challenges that put us in line for a bolstering phone call or coffee date with someone who loves us. Frequently, these old friends are listed as being useful to remind you about the old you, and to draw you away from talk about nappy rash and sleepless nights; but more importantly, these friends will be able to share opinions about wider, worldlier issues too, keeping you abreast and engaged with politics, culture and, of course, all those fabulous films you're now not getting out to see! The important thing to remember about people who are in a different stage of life from you is that there is more that connects you than disconnects you. You are going through fleeting stages of the parenthood cycle that they will not be able to relate to – pregnancy, birth, babies, toddlerdom, threenagers, school kids, teens, empty nesting – but they will be able to relate to your love of discovering great coffee shops, Ian McEwan novels, the films of Hugh Grant, glamping. You are more alike than you think, even if they roll their eyes when you mention your pinworm paranoia.

Quality not quantity

Having a wide circle of buddies is fun, but we all need a handful of friends who are there through thick and thin, and who we can count on when we're not feeling our most sparkly and charming.

These are the people we need to relish and cherish more than anyone else. How can we build upon these deep friendships?

- Nurture existing friendships by being the kind of friend you'd like others to be for you. Friendship is like an emotional bank account: you can't just make withdrawals and stay in the clear. Invest time, loyalty, support and ideas. Give this relationship value.
- Have fun together. Misery loves company, and especially in the trying days of motherhood, it can be an automatic response to meet mamas in a similar situation and moan about the lack of sleep and useless husbands, but that can only get you so far. Share your problems, but then head to the theatre or a concert, or ban talk of kids after the first hour.
- Open up and be honest. Authenticity bonds like nothing else. If you're putting up a wall, it'll be hard for the wonderful, sweet, clever people you want to attract and keep in your life to climb over to you. Share frustrations and embarrassing anecdotes, and ask real questions about things that concern you. Putting on a show is a no-go for meaningful connections.
- Show you can be trusted. Keep a secret and keep your mouth shut. Never say anything or write anything about a friend you wouldn't want them to see or overhear.
- Be available. Set dates and keep them. Check in if you know that they're going through something. Help when you can: watch their kids, offer a ride, take a snack.
- Get creative in your giving. If you see something a friend would love or it reminds you of them, treat them. Don't wait for a birthday. Give an IOU for a home-cooked dinner. Leave flowers or soup on the doorstep if they're sick. Treat them to bath oils when you know they're stressed. Bake treats for their family on a rainy day. Lend them a book

you've just finished and loved. Be the friend who is generous in spirit not just money.

- Show kindness to the people they care about. Welcome the
new partners of your recently divorced friends, until they
give you a reason not to, even if you liked the old ones. This
will make change easier for them, and their children. Invite
your friend's new mama mates on a night out; this will help
your buddy connect the different dots in her life, and you
could meet some interesting new people with new perspectives as well.

- Be the first to apologise. I hurt my oldest friend once, pre-kids,
in our early twenties. We didn't speak for two years and my
heart ached for her. After my pointless resistance to say sorry,
I wrote her what can only be described as a love letter, explaining and apologising. She agreed to meet me. I said sorry again
in person and she forgave me. This was twenty years ago.
We're now godmother to each other's children, we holiday
together every year and remain a key figure in each other's
lives. I'm so grateful that I gathered the guts to apologise.

- Be a good listener. Show interest in their day, too. Pay attention, follow up and remember details. I am always touched
when a friend asks about a throwaway comment I've made
or gets in touch to ask how an event went. When a friend
says something, it's because they want you to hear it.

Compete with your best self, not your girlfriends

At high school, I was jealous of the girls whom all the boys fan-
cied. In my first few jobs, I would get eaten up inside when the
bosses had their favourites who could do no wrong, ignoring my
conscientiousness and enthusiasm. Being pushed to the sidelines

never feels good, and if we allow it to, it can make rivals of people we would otherwise adore. Around the age of 30, I decided to focus on beating my own standards and setting my own targets, finally acknowledging that jealousy is a wasted emotion and that we're all starting from different levels and cannot be compared. Life, I realised, is a long race, and you're only truly competing against yourself – your best self – and no one else. I stopped looking out and started looking in.

I've witnessed many promising mama friendships collapse when jealousy has reared its ugly head. Nowhere is envy more destructive and depressing than in the realm of mothering, as some women seem to take to raising kids easier than others – and raise kids who *appear* to be (or we're constantly told are!) perfect, gifted, talented and all round wonderful, while yours ... not so much. At a time when we should be lifting each other up, *Schadenfreude* can make us feel an itchy, dirty joy when our friends' lives get a bit tricky, or when that dream child stumbles a little. This is unhealthy, mamas – unhealthy! There's enough good stuff to go around for everyone, and taking pleasure in another's bad times will make you feel bad deep down. A friend getting back to her pre-pregnancy weight doesn't mean you can't – it means you now have someone on hand to motivate and advise you. A friend's kid making the football team doesn't mean your kids can't, it means he has someone to practise with.

When a twinge of jealousy arises now (so-and-so's son is reading better than my son, or my daughter hasn't been invited to a party that everyone else seems to have), I face it directly. Why do I feel lesser? How can I feel better? And when people display jealousy towards me in the form of a backhanded compliment or subtle undermining, I acknowledge how it made me feel, store it in my brain as a warning bell, wish them well and move on. Buddha's last words were 'strive on diligently' and that is what I try to focus on: building good karma and concentrating on my own thoughts and actions, which

I can control, rather on the thoughts and actions of others, which I can't. I push towards my own personal and parenting goals with passion and determination, looking around me at other mothers only for inspiration, ideas and advice – never to crow or boast. You can land on your behind with egg on your face if you do that.

Nobody's perfect

Underneath the shine of a carefully curated external life, everyone has their doubts and insecurities; if you knew the full story you probably wouldn't feel jealous at all. Having a new car or a big house or a hot husband *does not* happiness make. Being comfortable in your own skin does; acknowledging what you have rather than what you don't does. Using your competitive spirit to spur yourself on and improve your own and your child's situation without worrying about someone else's does.

Mama says: Claire, 34

'When I became a mum, I had *no* mum friends. Not one. In the months leading up to my delivery, I started pre-natal yoga. Every class would begin with the teacher having us introduce ourselves, giving our due date and sharing a positive or negative thing from our pregnancy that week. About a month before my son arrived, another mom approached me and invited me to a "March mums' dinner". She had met a few other women due in March and wanted us all to get together and visit. We met for dinner for the first time while still pregnant, then kept an email chain updating each other when our babies arrived, with their gender and how our delivery went. We were all expecting "natural" births, and to our shock half of us had C-sections, and it was good to know that. We met again when our littles were four weeks old, and frequently throughout our maternity leave, sharing stories of breastfeeding,

postpartum depression, exhaustion and laughing about our first
time having sex again after giving birth ... *ouch!* No topic was off
limits, and these women became, and still are, my family.'

Parent Teacher Association paradise?

There's a cultural myth banded around that PTA mums are
like grown-up versions of the horrors from Mean Girls. Don't
listen. Annoying people exist everywhere; they're not disproportionately conditioned to take roles within your school's
parent–teacher association. The PTA meeting is not like a coven
of witches who busy themselves with cake baking instead of
spell stirring. Some will be authoritarian power-hungry monsters
but most just care about their kid and their kid's school. Like
you. Most feel a bit out of it and want to make friends with similar interests. Like you. If you have the time, get involved.

Joining my son's school's PTA not only helped me get to
know the priorities and concerns of the school better, it gave
me a plethora of knowledgeable parents with children in other
grades who could offer me advice. As I made friends with
these parents, my son made friends with their offspring –
giving him the kudos of saying hello to older kids in the school
corridor. Being part of the PTA also helps you to get to know
the teachers better. While they may not become friends, you'll
probably find them less intimidating or distant.

Pint-sized play dates

One crucial element in making the time for new mama friendships
is finding a way to make your time together fun for you and your

kids, and meeting fellow parents you adore whose offspring bond with yours. You can gossip while they play, with limited moaning. Don't force anything, but if they get on, nurture it: make meet-ups a regular part of your routine (children have short memories, and a regular routine will keep them connected) and plan fun activities, either arts-and-crafts projects at home or adventures outdoors.

If you don't like your friends' kids, don't make it into a big deal. Do not criticise them to your friend – there will be no quicker way to fall out. Shift your arrangements around so that you see her without forcing your kids together. Take some time out from the dates en masse, then try again. Kids are people, remember: going through hard times and rough patches that make them flare up and misbehave sometimes, but this is not who they always are or will be.

If you don't like your kid's friends, trust your gut. If you have a reason to think they are a bad influence on your child, keep them apart. Don't shout and yell, but subtly move them in a new direction, setting up play dates with other children they like, or allowing them to join new clubs or take up new hobbies they've shown an interest in.

Kids should be encouraged to nurture friendships in different groups, so they are not too invested in one particular friend or social circle, and less likely to fall victim to changing whims or in-crowds. As well as finding friends in school, they need to seek them in their street, their clubs, with their sibling's friends' siblings, and with family friends. If they invest time and affection in little pockets in different areas of their lives, they won't feel as vulnerable if one group is giving them a hard time, disbanding, or collapsing.

If they have any unsavoury friendships, you can use these as a way to teach them how to handle different personality types, disappointment or bullies. There are lessons for children to learn about forgiveness and kindness when they're confronted with peers who treat them badly. As a last resort, remember that this child will probably *not* end up as your son's best man or daughter's chief bridesmaid. Your child probably has good judgement too – if not now, then soon. Trying to take control over their social circle could push them towards the bad influence even more forcefully, so offer your opinion and share stories from your own childhood, and work out together the values you look for in a friend, and what you both deserve.

Band of brothers . . .

. . . or sisters! Setting up an environment where siblings can become good friends is a must-have for a happy home. My brothers are my best friends, the only people who truly understand my past, my parents, how we fit in the world and what we value in our homes and hearts. That love can never start quickly enough – but it can be tricky. My children currently have a love–hate thing going on. They miss each other when they're apart and can make each other laugh like no one else, but some days they bicker constantly, fighting over everything from the remote control to who is my favourite child. I tell them I love them equally, but that doesn't mean I have to treat them exactly the same, and pay them compliments at exactly the same time. Each one has to feel secure that they are equal, but accept that some days will be more about William and some more about Matilda. This reassurance helps them to live less like rivals and more like comrades.

How can you help them to get along? You can remember that each child is unique and comparing them is futile. Avoid discussing their differences in front of them and, when offering praise, pitch it in the language of a specific accomplishment rather than in being better than their sibling. Set ground rules for the behaviour you expect in your home, which applies to all, and encourage teamwork with praise and rewards. Finally, however hard it is to listen to their fighting and pestering, try to avoid getting stuck in the middle as much as possible. Let them find their own middle ground and solutions. If you take a side, the victor will feel smug and the loser will feel less loved and misunderstood. If one is clearly being the perpetrator, take them to one side to discuss their negative behaviour without the other one sticking their nose in.

Getting your partner on your side

In the game of parenting, no friendship is more important than the one you have with your co-parent. You really are the joint heads of your tribe, and so you need to be on the same side. Sometimes this is difficult, as Stadlen points out in *How Mothers Love: And How Relationships Are Born*. 'When both parents feel tired and uncertain, instead of supporting one another, both sometimes try to feel better by demoralising the other one, in a kind of competition to be a better parent.' As I read this my head shouted, 'No, no, no!' but in reality, there have been occasions when my husband and I have battled about what we feel is right – sometimes, in front of the kids, which is never good – desperate to get our way, or just to make the other person feel useless. This is not constructive or kind, and not good for anyone, especially our children.

When I'm tempted to criticise their father now, I've trained myself to stop and ask why. Do I want to smirk or scold because it will help our family unit, or because I'm frustrated about something else? Is he really being annoying on purpose, or does he genuinely not know where I've decided to keep their swimming goggles? Too often, I undervalue what my husband brings to our gang in a resentful burst of 'woe is me'. Too often, he does the same. We have got better at saying thank you to each other, and allowing each other more free time to pursue our own interests and goals outside the family, which then means we adults return to the home refreshed and reinvigorated, eager to share our news of the outside with the people who matter most.

Listen up, Buttercup!

A major gripe in relationships is that one partner – or both – feel they are not heard. Become a better listener by putting away distractions and focusing on what your partner is saying – not just the words but with their body language, facial expressions and tone of voice. Show interest and sympathy (even if you have to fake it just a little bit) and offer kind words and a hand to hold, rather than rushing them to conclusions and solutions. Don't interrupt or change the subject, instead allow them to get everything off their chest. When they ask for your input, give it – as you would give it to a friend – with kindness.

Teamwork makes the dream work

At the root of every family is the desire to succeed: as individuals and as a team. With this in mind, we share goals and ambitions, and we have each other's backs. It's hard adding children to a relationship. The intimacy and freedom you enjoyed is removed, and you are now two stretched, exhausted, scared adults trying to protect little people you love to the point of madness, often unable to articulate to the other your sense of confusion. Honesty is good in this situation. Calm conversations about shared values and new ideas can rebuild solidarity. Don't expect things to be easy or perfect, your relationship is changing, your priorities shifting. Your once leisurely life of selfishness has now sunk into a new world of early mornings and irrational fears. Ignore the gushing lovefest some people post on social media about dreamy dates and subservient husbands. A little digging under the surface will show things are not 100 per cent perfect for any of us, unfortunately. Be happy for those couples who seem to have pulled through tough times (ask for tips!) but refuse to get caught up in comparisons or criticism.

It's hard work. All of it – parenting *and* partnerships – and you have to know where your limits lie. Work out the truly bad stuff and where you are setting your goalposts from the unintentional niggles, grinds and annoyances found in all couples, and commit to working together. Getting through these trying times, with kindness and patience, will benefit you and your children – after all, no one in the world loves your child with as much passion and selfless devotion as your partner. Value them as you would a good friend.

Mama says: Sasha, 40

'When we moved into a new house, my neighbour, whom I had never met, came to my door and pleaded that I come to her house with my kids. She had four children and was desperate for a mum friend. I didn't know it at the time, but so was I. My kids and I stopped at her house at 2pm that afternoon and went home at 9pm that night. Her house was a mess, we fed our kids frozen pizza and let them watch TV and I realised that perfect was no longer my goal: happy was, because happy mums raise really good human beings. It was the most important friendship I have ever made. We now live on opposite sides of the country, but every week I look forward to texts about hilarious mishaps. My advice to any mum anywhere is to find the mum that is the least like you on the surface and you will learn so much – about yourself, about parenting and about not giving a s**t about perfection.'

Your PG rating

Write down your aims and think about these ideas as you move forward using this rating system.

The Ps:

Purpose What values do you look for in friends? Who do you want to attract?

Perspective How would your friends describe you? What could you improve?

Presence Whose friendship lifts your spirits today? Who brightens your life?

▶

The Gs:

Gratitude As you leave a get-together with a friend, tell them how thankful you are for them.

Goals Make a new friend this month, or nurture a relationship that has got waylaid in the business of motherhood.

Going for it Plan two events with friends – one with kids and one just for adults. Both should make your heart sing.

TAKE A DEEP BREATH, MAMA

Be a friend to yourself. You are your most reliable ally. How would you tell a friend to look after themselves, how would you make a friend feel better? 'You rock,' you'd say. 'I'm so proud of you!' You'd encourage them to take a bath, take a break, take that extra scoop of ice cream without feeling guilty. Tell that to yourself. Be your own BFF and you'll be a better friend to those around you.

8

Set Your Own Expectations

'This is one of the weird things about motherhood. You can predict that some of your best moments will happen around the toilet at six am while you're holding a pile of fingernail clippings like a Santeria priestess.'

Tina Fey, Bossypants

I assumed that I'd find motherhood easy. After all, I was desperate to have children and, after suffering three miscarriages, carrying, holding and nurturing my own child became my only goal, one that if I ever reached it, I imagined I'd feel nothing but gratitude and awe for. I also assumed that I had the disposition to be a great mama. I'd run a team of 50 people when I was the editor-in-chief of a magazine in New York, I'd completed impossible tasks on tight deadlines when I was a writer for a newspaper in London. Nothing fazed me. I could multitask, cope with late nights and temper tantrums, get stuff done. The circumstances were right, too: I was in my mid-thirties when William arrived, I had a supportive partner, a home, my health. Becoming a mother would be a breeze, surely.

It wasn't. I didn't understand the tsunami of emotions hitting me every day. I'd longed to be a mother for five years, so why was I not loving it as much as I thought I would? I was finding the day-to-day organisation and lack of sleep impossible, so was I doing something wrong? The first year of motherhood was spent backtracking, questioning, whining and crying. I was experiencing a magical love like no other, but there was no contented glow, saintly halo or maternal know-ingness. I assumed becoming a mother would turn me into a domestic goddess, a cook worthy of a place in the *Great British Bake Off* final, a Mary Poppins-style embodiment of loveliness and justice. Instead, I was the same old me: just a grey-faced, pinhole-eyed, baggy-leggings-wearing, second-guessing-myself version.

Feeling the pressure

When I had the time to analyse why I was feeling doubtful about my own skills and instincts as a mother, I realised that much of it came from the cacophony of judgement that surrounded me and surrounds all modern mothers. We do not get the time to be at peace with our child in our home. Opinions and voices shout at us from our phones, televisions and computer screens. We still have a village, but it is no longer just of village of friends, family and neighbours who know us, see us and want to help us, it is a global village of strangers who are all vying to shout the loudest, get hits, build a platform. These voices have a secondary effect when parents within our orbit quote them, copy them or boss you about using advice that, even if well-meaning, does not suit your aims and goals or your child's needs.

A good friend of mine, who I admire greatly for her lack of school-gate drama and engagement, and I were discussing this recently. 'I've just removed myself from the high expectations that are evolving around hectic parenthood,' she said. 'Listing our chores, invitations, commitments – it has a sort of one-upmanship that I can't engage with, this link between your level of parenting stress with your level of parenting involvement. My kids and I need quiet time, so I keep my expectations simple.' She made me realise that I can say yes too often, putting on that fake martyr act that so many of us do. There is no glory in burnout, only jangling nerves.

Step away from competition

How can you turn off this exterior pressure and set your own expectations? Don't engage in the 'I'm busier than you' game, competing over who has the most parties, sports classes or homework assignments on their calendar. We're all busy, we all have different coping mechanisms. There is no glory in taking on too much. A recent survey of 2,000 Belgian parents published in the *Frontiers in Psychology* journal discovered that 12.9 per cent of mothers were suffering with 'high burnout', leaving them exhausted, less productive and emotionally withdrawn at least once a week. Instead of celebrating the martyrdom of burnout, something I've noticed more and more in my conversations in person and online with other mothers, reject it and correct it. Just because you're not as busy as other mothers say they are, it doesn't mean that you're not working as hard or you are not as needed or as popular. It means that you are using your best judgement: saying no to unnecessary events or demands, prioritising sleep and self-care, refusing to engage in the 'I have such high expectations' game and quietly going about your business. Your children don't need a superhero. They need a mum.

Mama says: Hattie, 35

'I often wake up and have to pinch myself when I see two little faces staring at me. It wasn't a dream – they really are mine! How lucky I am – apart from the sleep deprivation, which is torture. I do everything I can to do the best for my babies and I still feel guilty. Did I spend enough time reading the library book? Did I rush off too soon at bedtime? Was I too grumpy when they dragged dinner out longer so that they could stay up later? Am I *enough* for them? I now live knowing that I have done everything I could to make life fun, I allowed them to be kids and I was present. I worked, but I made time that was just for them. Presence was a priority.'

How to boost your self-belief

To set your own expectations successfully, you need to have a self-assured attitude. How can you get one of those? You gotta have faith.

Conjure up confidence using visualisation techniques. Imagine yourself as a person to be proud of, give yourself a pep talk, look in the mirror and give the thumbs-up. Ask questions and allow your best self to answer them; for example, 'Why am I a great mum?'

Fake it until you make it Boost your self-confidence by looking after your exterior, and your interior will soon match. Dress nicely, not necessarily expensively, and it will put a spring in your step. Think about your posture and stand tall. Smile and your spirit will lift.

Be at your physical, mental and emotional best by getting good sleep, eating well, taking invigorating walks outside, and cutting down on the negative behaviours that leave you puffy, groggy or guilty. A 2016 study in *Neuropsychiatric Disease and Treatment* proved that regular physical activity and a healthy lifestyle improved body image, which made the participants feel more confident in all aspects of their life.

Don't allow your inner critic to flourish – stop the negative voice in your head. You can reframe your thinking by appreciating your successes (compliment, congratulate and reward yourself for jobs well done) or, if your inner critic is refusing to shut up, by talking to a therapist.

Stand up for equality You are just as good as everyone else. Other mothers you might see and worry about are no better, more deserving or successful than you. You are enough – the devil on your shoulder needs to accept that.

Give yourself and your family the best chance of success: be organised, be thoughtful, and plan. You will be able to meet your expectations if you have a clear agenda, realistic goals and a can-do attitude. Write a to-do list to help you focus, then write a did-it list to reinforce how capable you are.

Display self-compassion Beating yourself up will only damage your self-belief and stop you from setting your own expectations. Be kind to yourself, laugh it off, and remember that not only is nobody perfect but also no one is paying that much attention to what you're doing anyway – they're too busy worrying about meeting their own expectations.

Six rules for setting your best expectations

1. **Narrow down your view** to just looking at you and
    your children. Clarify what *you* want to teach them,
    show them and pass on to them, and forget about
    someone else's expectations or what they think is
    perfect, or even passable. Asking yourself questions will
    help to set your intentions and focus your attention.

2. **Spring clean your expectations regularly** Think about
    what has worked and what hasn't, what you'd like more
    or less of, then tinker your goals to suit. You don't have
    to commit to anything except the goal of contentment
    and peace.

3. **Throw the expectations forced onto you from your
    past** in the bin. What your parents wanted you to be,
    what your school teachers told you you'd become –
    enough! You're the adult now. You get to decide. Break
    out of the old mould you were squeezed into – the
    messy child, the nervous child, the bossy child – and
    design your own sense of who you are and how you
    want to raise your family.

4. **Don't get hung up on the details** that make your
    expectations of perfection impossible. Think from your
    kids' perspective. You might want to make everything
    photo-adorable and neat, but does your child care if
    he has a hole in his jeans, or you forgot to brush his
    hair, or the cake you ordered for his birthday party
    is chocolate but you ordered vanilla? Of course not!

If he is disappointed that something has gone awry,
sympathise, don't dramatise, then find a way to laugh
about it.

5. **Don't confuse high expectations with happiness**
   Don't beat yourself up if you're not packing elaborate
   organic lunch boxes or planting a vegetable garden.
   You are not being lazy or unambitious for your family.
   You are being kind to yourself. Your child would rather
   have a chilled-out, calm mum in the morning than a
   homemade lentil soup and fresh bread for lunch. Trust
   me.

6. **Be brave** Say no, say yes, change your mind – while
   being considerate. We often make decisions from the
   position of fear: what will they think of me? What
   if it goes wrong? What if I'm not enough? Take a
   deep breath, go for a walk, have a warm bath and set
   expectations for you and your family from a mindset
   of confidence and courage, the opposite of doubt and
   dread.

Causing a commotion

Some people are just mean. There is never a justifiable
reason for anyone to criticise your post-baby body, your
relationship with your partner, or your method of finding a
work–life balance. If someone drops an insult (or a truth
bomb) without you asking for it, you are perfectly within your
rights to ignore it, expose it for the harsh hit that it is, or to
fight back with every verbal bone in your body. No one has

▶

the right to make your feel lesser. But, still the judgement can flow. Watch out for the big parenting dilemmas and questions that you need to stand firm on. I was amazed at the amount of unasked-for opinions that I was offered on all the topics below, and the passion with which they were shared with me – even by strangers! Some people are downright hostile if people disagree with them, and I've found it best – when confronted with a gung-ho advocate of this or that – to 'interview' them rather than talk about yourself and your child. Ask how they came to their decision, why they've set their expectations as they have and how it's going for them. Deflect politely, and use their information to either confirm or question your own expectations. Be prepared. Hot topics, listed here in the order you'll face them, include:

- C-section versus natural birth
- Drugs or drug-free birth
- Circumcising a boy or not
- Breast versus bottle
- Vaccinations or not
- Attachment parenting versus letting a child 'cry it out'
- When to start giving the baby real food and how to wean
- When – or if – to return to work
- How and when to potty train
- How to handle public tantrums
- When – if – you should start considering your next pregnancy
- How to discipline your child
- If they should go to private or state school
- If you should force them to do sports
- When and how you should tell them about sex
- How much pocket money to give
- Making them help around the house or not
- When to let them go out on their own, and how late

▶

There is no one-size-fits-all answer to any of these oft-debated parenting conundrums. No universal right or wrong, although, of course, the world is full of big mouths who think it's their way or the highway. It can be infuriating to face criticism for your choices from people close to you, like your own parents, and embarrassing to get tutting and sidelong glances from strangers. And so, trusting in your own expectations is perhaps the area of motherhood that requires you to out-Zen yourself the most. Quieten those critical outside voices and have faith in your instincts. Contemplate your own unique route to a balanced, happy family home while dropping the illusion that you can, or would want to, people-please or pretend to be perfect.

As easy as 1–2–3

A warm and wise wellness instructor I was lucky enough to meet recently was worried about the level of frazzled energy among the mamas in a retreat she was leading. 'Sometimes it's hard to see solutions and focus on your own expectations and abilities when you're in the middle of a rainstorm,' she said, 'even if you know this time will have to end eventually. So, I'm going to share my strategy for keeping my sh*t together. And it's easy.' She then outlined her method of setting her own realistic expectations of herself and what she could achieve. She explained it was her first stop in self-care and she called it her 1–2–3 strategy. When she is feeling overwhelmed or lethargic, she follows this path to feeling better and getting stuff done. Breaking her chores and aims into bite-sized chunks with clear expectations brings her balance and confidence.

1. Do something you have to do: when your brain or body is stopping you from doing the multitude of tasks you have to tick off your to-do list, pick one and mentally shift your attitude from a 'threat state' (when the pressure you feel stops your brain from operating at its peak) to a 'challenge state' where you see the one task as a chance to conquer something.

2. Do something you want to do: you've got the hard part out of the way in part 1, so now you deserve to prioritise *you*. Rewarding yourself, studies show, boosts overall motivation in all aspects of your life. This second stage will reboot your brain and boost your happiness.

3. Do something for someone else, even small actions can boost your happiness, research proves, so volunteer, buy a gift, listen to a friend. Helping others analyse their emotions and dramas can help you to understand yours, too.

Mama says: Jo, 47

'I feel that society pushes us to have unrealistic expectations for our children and leaves mothers feeling like failures if they don't have these "perfect kids". I read somewhere that you want your children to make all the mistakes that they can under your roof so that they can learn from their mistakes when they have a loving support system at home. All we should want for our kids is for them to be happy and passionate about something. And if you want your kids to be kinder, sweeter and have better manners, model that behaviour. Kids get there at their own time. I remember my son being the last to walk, to be fully potty trained, to ride a bike. I envisioned myself carrying him to school, packing a pull-up in his backpack and him parking his tricycle in the senior school bike rack. What I learned was not to rush anything; they evolve at their own pace. Our panic and fear won't change anything.'

Can you keep it in the family?

When it comes to setting your own expectations, it might be your parents who stand most firmly in your way. Perhaps you'll want to replicate the traditions and pastimes your parents pursued when you were a child now that you're a mama. Maybe you won't. Times have changed, you parent differently, your children have different interests and friends from the ones you had. You could be living a different life, in a different way, in a different city or country. Perhaps your mother stayed at home to look after you whereas you work full-time, perhaps your parents were divorced whereas you're still trying to make it work with your partner.

When it comes to plunging into your past, the key is to take the bits you loved that you can make work and ditch the bits that don't fit into your world. And don't let the besotted grandparents take away, judge or interfere to the point that it infuriates you or your partner, or encroaches on their relationship with their grandchild, which should be treasured and protected at all costs.

Grandparents are brilliant, most of the time, loving your children as much as you do and helping you care for them. Set expectations and guidelines around this multi-generational relationship to limit friction and misunderstanding:

Focus on the positives: grandparents interfere because they care. Don't be too defensive about every suggestion they make. Choose your battles. My mother tells me she still sees *me* as *her baby*, and wants to look after me, which sometimes can come across as telling me what to do, but always from a place of love and protection.

Being a grandparent is the fun reward for surviving the parenting years. If your parents don't follow your rules about napping, sugar and television once a month when they're giving you a free-babysitter date night, don't chew them out. Remind them of your wishes in a non-confrontational way after the event, politely and gently. Your child will survive, but if you don't take this route, your relationship and cheap babysitting service may not.

Never fight or disrespect each other in front of the grandchild. They're watching and picking up on how parents interact with their children, and vice versa from you lot – you're their role models. When big lines have been crossed, calmly take the grandparents to one side and ask for their support. Explain that you know that they are acting with love but that a certain expectation is important to you. If you catch them again, don't give up. Confront them, calmly, again and say that it's a real deal breaker for you and you're politely asking them to stop. If they refuse, you'll have to rearrange your relationship to maintain a bond but that doesn't allow them a free hand with things important to you.

Educate your parents on how things have changed Invite them along to play dates so that they can hear from other parents, buy them modern grandparenting books, email them relevant articles that you've enjoyed that reflect your expectations. Don't preach, just provide opportunities for them to set new rules. But don't dismiss their years of hands-on experience raising kids. After all, you turned out all right, didn't you?

Let them form unique bonds that play to their strengths. My mother loves history and the arts, so we have a once-a-year tradition that she takes my two around a London landmark then to a West End show. It's a thrilling day for all, and it allows them to connect over shared interests.

All of these points apply for your in-laws too – and don't be afraid to be the one to bring concerns up if you think you'd handle it better or quicker, or with less fireworks, than your partner.

How to harness happiness: the highs and lows

Possibly my expectations of motherhood were too high. I naively imagined that with the birth of my son I would feel complete. I thought that I'd be a natural. I thought that I'd be able to continue my life as it was, just with a cute appendage. In the first year I felt frustrated that I couldn't work when I wanted to and that I had to put someone else's needs before my own 24/7. As he got older – and started walking, talking and fighting with me – my time and brain space felt even more constricted. Adding his baby sister was double the trouble.

How did I refocus my expectations of myself, my career and my happiness to fit around my new role? I lived in the present, not worrying about the future, which I couldn't control, and I took more pleasure in the day-to-day accomplishments and successes: a giggling fit, an uninterrupted conversation with a friend, a hike in the woods. I started to see myself as two separate entities: as a mother and as a woman, and kept an eye on both versions of *me*. I checked that neither side of me was feeling too neglected, or if one was, I remembered that it was short-term and that if I was perfect, I'd have nothing to strive for. I labelled my emotions and shared them with my husband and friends ('I'm feeling lonely', 'I'm feeling bored') and listened to their ideas about how to shake it off. I adapted to my new situation day by day, remembering that I wanted this, and replacing the negative moan of 'I have to' with 'I get to': I get to go to a mummy-and-me music class, I get to make my babies breakfast, I get to go on this great journey with little people I love.

Gender expectations and labels

Eliminating gender stereotyping – or not! – is society's current expectation obsession. As a child, I was such a tomboy that I insisted my name was Richard until I was five. My daughter, on the other hand, has never seen a unicorn, cupcake, glitter paint or doll's dress that she hasn't loved and fawned over. She is the girliest, girliest girl. This means that I face judgement as she parades alongside me in public with a rainbow handbag slung over her arm, bangles jangling on her wrist, inseparable from Willa, her dolly – who often wears matching bangles. A year ago, fed up with being socially embarrassed, I moaned to my husband. 'Where has she come from? Why does she talk about her appearance so much? I am not girly. I don't go out of my way to make her like this. I give her Lego, balls, books without princesses in!' I said, exasperated that Matilda had once again asked to perform a fashion show for us, then spent the rest of the morning folding blankets for her baby. 'It comes from within her,' my husband replied. 'She likes what she likes. I don't know why you worry.'

I knew why. It was because people who didn't know me or my daughter were telling me that I was doing her a disservice, that I couldn't be a feminist if I had a daughter with a toy kitchen. My husband made me get a grip and I have learnt to shrug off remarks about gendering my child, which are normally made by non-parents, or parents with children too young to choose their own toys and interests. I offer gender-neutral toys, books, films and television shows to my son and daughter, and I have stopped feeling like some stereotypical pusher from the 1950s because of just what my husband says: children are their own people, and they deserve acceptance, however pink or blue or multi-coloured their interests are.

As long as both sexes know they should value the universal qualities of kindness, honesty, empathy and loyalty (which are not gender markers) and there is no talk of a girl being weaker than a boy, or of it being less acceptable for a boy to show his emotions than a girl, I am happy to accept that Matilda is happier playing with her kitchen than with a tractor. As long as she sees healthy role models around her – between me and her dad, at home and at work, or between her teachers at school – I don't mind if she desperately wants a Barbie for her birthday. I will continue to let my boy child and girl child play as they wish, displaying a full range of emotions and interests, and treating them as individuals rather than a positive or negative stereotype. Our expectations should be towards balance, fairness and equality, not forcing a child to squash his or her instincts.

Your PG rating

Read and react to the lists below, then jot down your own take on the topics and how you can make them work for you and your family in the future.

The Ps:

Purpose Write a list of the expectations you have for yourself and your family.

Perspective Turn off the outside noise, and focus on what will make you and your children flourish. Be clear and realistic in your philosophy.

Presence Remember that even when things don't go to plan, your child should never feel like a disappointment, and you should never feel like a failure.

The Gs:

Gratitude Distil the inspiration from the outside world and the influence of your own childhood into a new blueprint for your best life. Be grateful for good ideas and experiences, and build upon them.

Goals Discuss and explain your expectations with your family. Listen to their needs and be adaptable. As your family evolves, so can your expectations, so keep an open dialogue and the possibility of change on the table.

Going for it Once you have set your expectations, commit to them, as a team.

TAKE A DEEP BREATH, MAMA

Your intuition as a mother is your most powerful tool on this journey, so slow down and listen to it. Your heart and head combined know what you and your family need, so stop second-guessing yourself. Admit your mistakes, then forgive them. Trust your gut. Trust yourself to set your own expectations. No one else could do a better job.

9

Make Peace with Your Critics

'Being a good mother does not mean being perfect every single moment. We screw up, we get mad, we drink too much, eat too much, yell too much.'

Amy Hatvany

I have a deep desire to be liked by everyone. My birth father never loved me, which left a father-shaped Freudian hole, a hole that I have been desperately trying to fill with strangers' affection and friends' approval since I was six years old. Being likeable, I guessed, would mean that I'd healed, I'd survived. So, being disliked – or even worse, being criticised or rejected – meant what? In my head it meant that my deepest fears were right: I was unlovable, unworthy. Now, as a parent myself, I can recognise that his failings had nothing to do with me. Actually, now, I realise that the positives of that painful experience were innumerable. Watching my mother flourish as a single parent taught me how a woman's resilience, courage and strength were undeniable, and watching my stepfather join our disrupted family with such generosity and kindness taught me how we can find love where love wants to live, and that men can be remarkable. I'd been focusing my whole life on the 'hole', what was missing, instead of what I'd gained. The day I became a parent, this all came into sharp focus. I needed to thank my mother and stepfather for all they'd *given* me and to stop beating myself up for what had been taken away. I needed to thank the people who loved me regardless and find a way to rid my brain of the anxiety caused by those who didn't.

Shifting my mind and its ability to cope with criticism or confrontation has been very, very hard and taken a lot of deep contemplation and self-analysis. Occasionally, it has also required a stern word with myself ('At least I know who my true friends are', 'Do they have a point?' and 'This is not about you; stop being so self-obsessed') or a pep talk from my husband, 'If they don't like you, it's their loss. They are missing out big time,' he'll say, confused by my fragile ego.

Amazingly, becoming a mother, which brings to the forefront so much hostile criticism, complaints and rude remarks, has actually *helped* me to get a grip on my own self-esteem. I'm filled with tiger blood. If I'm going to protect my offspring, I need to protect myself too. And that means from harmful verbal assaults, unkind actions or from self-flung arrows finding chinks in my mental armour. I never did believe that 'sticks and stones' song we were taught in the playground. Criticism hurts and we need to build a strong defence against it.

Are you your own worst critic?

Too often, the worst offender when it comes to being criticised and ridiculed is oneself. Women, especially, are trained to diminish their accomplishments, refuse compliments, look for faults and over-share failings. There are ways to shift this damning mindset to a neutral one. I am not suggesting for one minute that any mama should turn into an ego maniac, I just want you to talk kindly, decently, to yourself.

If your mind starts scrambling to a place of *can't, won't, don't,* call it out. Why is your inner critic scared or worried? Be honest with yourself, assess the safety aspects of each pursuit, thank your inner critic for being concerned, and go ahead if it really is right for you.

Celebrate your successes, and acknowledge your defeats with an honest appraisal of what you could do differently next time. Don't let these failures lurk in dark, lonely places – bring them out into the open so that your inner critic can't sneak up on you with cruel whispers. Accept that you can't always win and that often it's the *trying* that teaches you the most and gives you the most pleasure.

If the voice in your head is too loud, talk to someone who you trust cares about you. Your inner critic distorts reality; an outsider can be honest but fair.

Keep an accomplishment journal List all the things you've done – big and small – that make you proud. Not in your head – I want this list where you can see it, read it and refer to it when you're suffering a self-esteem tumble. Doing something every day that scares you is an old classic, and it doesn't have to be jumping out of a plane – it could be swimming outside, saying hello to a fellow parent at the school gates or picking up a challenging book. Note down all these things. As the list grows, so will your inner confidence.

If your inner critic still keeps talking, be rude back. 'Yeah, yeah, I've faced worse haters than you. My ex-boss said *blah, blah, blah* about me, and my school teacher said *jabber, jabber, jabber*. Do your worst, weird, rude inner voice! You don't scare me! You're just some whining hangover from my insecure teenage years that is sticking around like a bad smell. I'm fierce now!'

How to avoid becoming a critical mother

Negatively appraising others is a form of bullying. Is it constructive? Will it help the person you're saying these things to? If you're just doing it to feel better about yourself, or to make a joke, or to win points with other antagonisers, stop it. Bullying is never cool, but to bully other mothers who are tired, depleted and full of self-doubt is as bad as bullying a child. Before opening your mouth, refer to that old saying, 'If you don't have anything nice to say, don't say anything at all.' Other ways to stop yourself being critical include:

- If a fellow mama asks for your honest opinion, do give it, but judiciously, with no dramatic embellishments. If you feel comfortable doing so, show her that you are on her side by sharing your own vulnerability. And don't discuss her drama with other people. Feel privileged that she came to you for advice, and keep her worries to yourself.

- If a family member or friend is constantly disappointing you, instead of critiquing them, adjust your expectations of who they are and what they do. This will soothe your frustrations and give you the power to accept their foibles, or to walk away without causing a scene. Readjusting your own thoughts and actions when dealing with their quirks gives you power.

- Being a critic will make you feel bad; remember that next time you're tempted to tut or give someone a dirty look. Train yourself to see the positives over the negatives. Yes, that woman may be blocking the entrance with her stroller, but good for her for getting out in the rain with her kids, she's sending another resilient little person out into our world.

- This is probably not about you. When people do things that you find annoying – that you want to have a go at them for, to their face or behind their back – try to see things from their side and don't take everything so personally. Everyone is stressed and overcommitted.

- Be upfront about what you expect from your relationships – calmly, respectfully and realistically. If it really winds you up that your friend is late to every meet-up, bring it up jokily and suggest an alternative: keeping play dates to your homes so that she can't keep you waiting in some random place; inviting other people along so that you aren't waiting alone; buying her an alarm clock. If this fails, go back to my previous point about readjusting your own expectations, and decide whether this friendship is worth the frustration.

Mama says: Chloe, 38

'Don't listen to the noise. One thing I don't do is care what other mothers think. I quickly learned that I would never survive if I did. Let them comment, let them advise you. Smile, thank them, and in your head tell them to go f*** themselves. Being a working mom (the juggle is real!) I often feel as if I get everything done *okay* but nothing done *well*. I have (mostly) learned to make peace with that. I start my day with four coffees to wake up and I wind down with two vodka tonics most nights. No one is going to say that this is a good idea, but it's what works for me. I have two under fives and two jobs – you do what you have to do.'

Move on from toxic friendships

Sometimes friendships don't turn out or develop in the way that we planned. A person you had high hopes for turns out to be *not* on your level. Perhaps they suck the energy out of you like a vampire; perhaps you've noticed that they don't have a good word to say about anyone else, leaving you insecure about what they are saying about you behind your back. Perhaps your supposed friend has become your biggest critic. Sometimes, things just don't gel and you find conversation a struggle, your meet-ups a strain rather than a joy. That's fine. We can't like all the people all the time – and sadly (I've found out through heart-breaking personal experience), some people just won't get you.

How, then, do you clear your diary for the people who make you feel enriched, excited and supported? Good advice a friend gave me a decade ago when I'd fallen into a vacuous group was to 'stay close to people who feel like sunlight': friends who show you warmth and brighten your day. Don't waste time with those who pull you into darkness. If you've given someone the benefit of the doubt for a time that feels right to you but it's not working, feel free to back off. The only way to win with a toxic person is not to play their game, so don't feel under pressure to spend your valuable spare time with someone who doesn't make you feel great when you're walking away from them. Some people, posing as friends, want to put you down, keep you down, and make you feel down about yourself. In the blur and constant questioning phase of new or early motherhood, you just don't need that. These people aren't necessarily nasty, just human, and you need to raise your friend-selection game.

How to improve the situation

You must take control of the relationship before it starts to eat away at your spirit. First, be upfront. Remind them that you are friends who are there to support each other, and if any of your changes have made them uncomfortable and distressed rather than happy for you, you can talk about it. Self-improvement can often bring out the worst in friendships – with one person becoming resentful of a positive change in the other, such as weight loss, a job promotion or finding new friends. Perhaps they could join you in your new positive attitude, rather than trying to bring you down. If the upfront approach doesn't work, or if it makes the situation worse, you need to respectfully back away. When you are improving your life, you need to surround yourself with people who love you, not those who feel embittered with anger or aggression towards you. As you become more self-confident, positive and aware of your values as a mother, you will naturally attract friends who bolster you rather than knock you down.

If cutting them out feels too harsh, just take more control. See them when *you* want to, not when they demand to. Learn to say no. Switch off your phone if they're blowing it up; block them from social media. Refuse to engage in negative talk about others. Stand up for yourself if you sense that they're trying to bully or criticise you or your parenting. Spend more time with people who make you feel good. This friendship still might feel like a cross you have to bear, but at least you won't lose your self-respect.

Cheer-up tunes

Walk away from your naysayers, give praise to your cheerleaders and believe in yourself by belting out these empowering and uplifting anthems:

'Roar' by Katy Perry

'Drag Me Down' by One Direction

'Born this Way' by Lady Gaga

'Control' by Janet Jackson

'Tough' by Goldroom

'Just the Way You Are' by Bruno Mars

'Shine' by Take That

'Not Ready to Make Nice' by The Dixie Chicks

'Shake It Off' by Taylor Swift

'This Is Me' by Keala Settle

Lastly, if a friend you treasured shuts you out of their lives, look at their reasons and your actions with a clear head and open heart. If you find anything wanting within yourself, change it. Become a better friend in the future. Send them good wishes and give them space. If you know in your heart that you didn't do anything wrong, mourn the loss and move on. As a clever mate told me recently, 'Don't feel sad over someone who gave up on you; feel sorry for them because they gave up on someone who would have never given up on them.' In friendships, as in love affairs, some you win and some you lose.

Respond, don't react

The greatest piece of advice I've ever been given about handling criticism, or even opinions that differ from yours, is learning to *respond* to what you've heard, rather than *reacting* to it. Taking this control of the situation will stop you from giving the other person power over you. It will stop you embarrassing yourself, or saying something you regret. It will allow you to grasp a healthy variety of perspectives without a closed mind. In these deeply diversified times, this piece of advice has helped me out with family, friends and strangers. When you respond, you have listened, you have thought it through, and you can firmly put your opinion out there or ask a question to challenge theirs. When you react, a red mist descends and common sense can go out the window.

Don't let the buggers grind you down – here are five steps for ignoring unwanted commentators:

1. **Start from a place of reality** Sometimes you're the rude person, so climb off that high horse. Being rude doesn't make you a bad person, it just means that sometimes you put your foot in your mouth, and this is

true of others too. Maybe they said it wrongly, or they thought you were more confident and resilient than you are because that is the aura you give out.

2. **Throw their criticism back to them** Stand up for yourself and say, 'I'm quite hurt by that. What do you mean?' and you'll probably get more information on their comment (that might be constructive) or on them (that they are insecure).

3. **Be objective** Do they have a point? Should you be letting your child walk barefoot around a restaurant where glasses get smashed? Should she be wearing a hat on a sunny day? Is she waving that stick too close to that smaller child's face? It's too easy to see ourselves or our children as perfect, but that's not realistic. There's always room for self-improvement.

4. **Dis the drama** People with goals and purpose don't engage with drama, they spend their time on things that add value to their lives and the lives of those they love. Be that person. Beware, however, that some people are just pillocks who like causing upset. To those people I want you to say, 'Cheerio – good luck with that attitude!' (under your breath, obvs) and walk away. Just because they're rude, you don't have to be. As Michelle Obama said, 'When they go low, we go high.'

5. **Fight critics with cordiality** If you can't walk away, give the person a chance to calm down, and stay friendly. When I've done this, the situation has not only chilled out, but it has also gone from one of attitude to gratitude. A mum friend once yelled 'You're

too bossy!' in a car park when I had reminded her of a
school commitment she needed to complete by the next
day. I was hurt, although I admitted to myself that I
can be bossy, and I could tell that she was embarrassed.
I didn't huff and puff or storm off. I said, 'I can be, and
I know you've got a lot on. I was trying to be helpful,
sorry,' and she had the chance to say sorry too, and we
are still great mates. If I'd overreacted or made it all
about me, we wouldn't be talking today.

Recognise good advice in bad conversations

When I say bad conversations, I mean hard conversations, or
weird interactions with strangers, which now you're a mama will
get more and more frequent. Firstly, feel the visceral vibe you get
from someone (look into their eyes) about whether they should be
heard. You do get warning bells about people – just make sure you
listen out for them. A couple of weird feelings from a new friend
recently left me feeling unsettled, and when I told an old friend
she said, 'I'm gonna just tell you what my wise grandma would
have said, "Don't mess with it, don't play with it"', which was
brilliantly succinct and useful for me to take on board because
it rang true. Before following someone's advice, consider the
source: do they have your best interests at heart, could they be
cheering for an opposing team? And always consider the risk of
taking advice, even if you asked for it: you are the only one who
will suffer the consequences. Good advice will sit nicely with
your heart and head, the giver's body language will be open, and
you will know that they have nothing to win or lose from what
they have said – apart from getting to spend time with a happier,
calmer you!

Mama says: Helena, 44

' "Pick your arguments" – my life became so much easier when a friend offered that simple piece of advice to me, and acknowledge that sometimes that advice also means with your-self. I used to be my biggest critic. I'd get upset if we were not going to have the most perfect day with the kids wearing the most perfect outfits, now I let it go. Sometimes my kids are my biggest critics, too, especially when I tell them that we're putting the electronic devices away and going out together. They soon stop moaning though, and I actually feel they experience a sense of relief that they have an excuse not to be stuck on their phones all day!'

Families – which size is wise for you?

People will feel the need to comment on many aspects of your parenting decisions, but, according to my friends who've made this choice (or had this choice thrust upon them), the decision to stop at one child is met with unrivalled criticism. *No sibling? He'll grow up weird and lonely, precocious and pretentious! Then he'll have the burden of you in old age with no help!* People are rude, aren't they? Friends who choose to have more than three children get told they are selfish over-breeders who are killing the planet. Unless you have 2.4 children, people will put their own issues on you, it seems. You know what you do? You do what you want. Share your story if you feel you can. What if you can't? You give them a chance to back off by changing the subject. If they continue, say that the decision is a private one and you'd rather not talk about it. If they are completely devoid of social etiquette and carry on, throw it back to them and say, 'Those are interesting ideas – how did you choose when to stop having kids?' If they continue, you are totally within your rights to walk away. There is no excuse in these times, when people are aware of infertility struggles or financial difficulties – and a woman's right to choose what is best for her body, life and career – for anyone to be judgemental about the choices you have made about the size of your family.

Turn your stress upside down

A yogi I know swears by the power of turning horrid moments on their heads – literally. When family drama gets too much, or your partner is being rude about your cooking and you want to slap him, remove yourself from the situation, lie down and stick your legs in the air. Rest them against a wall, or rest your hips on a block or pillow and hold them aloft for ten minutes. The effect is calming and relaxing, and blood will reflow around your frustrated body. If your kids are the source of your frustration, get them to join you. They will think you're crazy fun, and feel the benefits, too. One friend has tried this in the changing room of a department store, another has done it in the dining room during a particularly irritating political debate on Christmas Day. Both swear it works.

Mama says: Emma, 29

'I will never forget this. I was having a really tough time breastfeeding my four-month-old after a lot of delivery and postpartum complications, plus colic. I went to a baby shop to buy nursing tank tops, something I didn't even know existed before motherhood. When I mentioned to the shop assistant my struggles with getting enough breast milk for my baby, her response was, "Well I hope you do not give the baby that poisonous formula." I was so exhausted and overwhelmed, I did not respond, but I soon realised what a cruel thing that was to say to a new mum. The comment stuck with me. Looking back, I wish I'd said, "I love my baby very much and however he gets his food is none of your damn business." But it took me a lot of time and reflection to realise that mothers should love and care for their babies how they see fit. This experience helped me support other new mums going through this struggle of breastfeeding versus bottle feeding.'

Start the day with confidence

Recent research uncovered by a team at University College London shows that it takes on average 66 days to form a habit, for a process to go from unnatural to automatic. I use this information to develop family customs that can bolster my children when dealing with critics. Sending your kids – your beating heart – out into the world is hard. Worrying about them being bullied or left out away from my watch has probably been my greatest fear as a mother, and developing these practices has probably helped me as much as them.

One routine we have got into has been starting our day with a confidence-boosting reminder of how loved they are. As I wake them up, I sit beside them, gently rubbing their backs and arms and saying, 'Let me squeeze some love into your bones, to keep you warm throughout the day!' My daughter says that she can feel it whooshing through her muscles and fortifying her for the day ahead. My son, who isn't so outwardly emotional, doesn't vocalise his need for this routine, but asks for a morning hug if I ever forget.

Another thing we have made standard at home is to always listen. 'Mama, can I tell you something?' Matilda will ask. 'Always. You can always tell me anything and we'll discuss it,' I reply, hoping that this instils in her the knowledge that she will always be heard at home, and I will support her through any inner questions or turmoil, regardless of any drama outside the home with people outside the family. And I listen. I make eye contact and show her that I can see her; I pause my television show, put down my phone.

These two simple acts have helped to create a strong foundation, which I hope will carry us through the teenage years, when a natural distancing between parents and children can allow negative outside influences to creep in. Building this physical and verbal bond with your kids can help you to identify the signs of bullying (if your child is acting differently, not eating, not sleeping, saying they dislike school, or mimicking unfriendly behaviour from outside within the home) and make it easier for them to come to you, knowing that they will be heard, supported and believed, and that you will be a team against their critics.

Mama says: Aimee, 30

'My ex-husband was two people: nice and not so nice. The life we'd made was not the one I deserved nor wanted, but I felt the pressure of society and other familial expectations that told me this was normal, that marriage was supposed to be this hard and that to divorce would be the absolute worst possible scenario for our child. So, I wanted to die instead. Thank God I finally woke up. Death is not the answer, choosing life is, and divorce can be a blessing. The clouds have lifted. I'm the mother I always wanted to be and I'm back to the person I once was: fun loving, caring and positive. I even have a relationship with my ex that is friendly and noncommittal, and I have no expectation other than for him to be a good and present father. I do not think of the past as a negative stain, because why waste the energy? What I went through has brought me immense understanding about what I want and need in this life. It also brought me the joy of being a mother to a wonderful child who is happy and healthy. I am strong and I am here, and this is my truth.'

Your PG rating

Use these suggestions to think about your own Ps and Gs and keep a note of what works.

The Ps:

Purpose To stop listening to critics and start listening to your own heart, head and gut.

Perspective Analyse input from outsiders – and its source – and take only what you need.

Presence 'Some people have a lot to say about me and my kids, but what do I want to say?'

The Gs:

Gratitude Be thankful for constructive criticism that comes from a good place, it will help you improve. Also, be thankful for your discernment in not taking on all comments.

Goals To tune out your inner critic. Stop being critical of others, and do not dwell on the outer critics who mean you harm.

Going for it Fight criticism with kindness – to yourself and others.

TAKE A DEEP BREATH, MAMA

If someone makes a mean comment or accusation about you or your children, flip the perspective and instead of burying it internally and allowing it to fester, push it back to them. My mother taught me when I was a young child and was being bullied by some girls in school that happy people don't say or do mean things. Scared people lash out through fear. Miserable people hurl insults to make others feel as miserable as them. Jealous people rain on a parade to feel temporarily superior. Decide which of these people is spewing their garbage at you, wish them well, and feel relief that you are not them.

Follow Your Unique Path to Happiness

'Remember that there is no happiness in having or in getting,
but only in giving. Reach out. Share. Smile. Hug. Happiness
is a perfume you cannot pour on others without getting a few
drops on yourself.'

Og Mandino

A wise woman once told me that life is 10 per cent what happens
to you and 90 per cent how you react to it. Life is at times hard,
confusing, painful, sad, tough, exhausting, depressing and difficult. Throwing children into the mix can make it more so. But
the fact that you've chosen to pick up this book, and you've got to
Chapter 10, proves to me – and it should prove to you, too – that
you're determined to create a calm, contented life the way *you*
want it to be and what your children need it to be. I have every
faith that you can and will take what is thrown at you (the 10 per
cent) and shape it into your best version of joy and tranquillity.

What is happiness? Since time began, the world's most inspiring philosophers and writers have agreed that it cannot be
bought, sold or given to you; it has to come from within, using a

Zen attitude of reducing the noise of outside opinions and looking within your heart to find and secure your own road to emotional fulfilment. 'Happiness does not consist in having what you want, but in wanting what you have,' believed Confucius. 'Happiness depends upon ourselves,' claimed Aristotle. 'The Constitution only gives people the right to pursue happiness. You have to catch it yourself,' warned Benjamin Franklin. These are great observations, from great men, but how does a modern mama, stretched by work, life, mental or physical health issues and negative societal influences, find enough happiness within herself for her own well-being and her family's? The first modern self-help guru, Dale Carnegie, devoted a whole chapter in his 1948 bestseller, *How to Stop Worrying and Start Living*, to cultivating a mental attitude that brings peace and happiness, declaring 'find yourself and be yourself (remember there is no one else on earth like you)'. Embracing your parenting uniqueness and your individual route to joy is the only authentic way to live, especially when motherhood can leave you depleted (putting others' needs before your own and worrying about your child's future) and restricted (the old routes to bliss – alone time, cocktails, spa days and lie-ins – are now impossible or infrequent).

How to be happy

Since I was a child, I've had the disposition of a rather serious person who finds it difficult to be light-hearted and silly. 'She's an old woman in a young girl's body,' a nursery school teacher told my mother when I was four years old and contemplating life, alone, looking out of the classroom window while the other children yelped and giggled around me. My contemplative nature might be interpreted as morose but, fundamentally, I am happy. I've had moments where I have been desperately unhappy, of course: when I was ostracised at school as a child, when I got my heart broken for the first time as a teen, when I felt like a failure asking for a divorce in my twenties, and when I lost longed-for pregnancies in my thirties. I have also had moments when I have felt low, lumpy and lethargic, when I have been dissed by friends, rejected for a promotion, argued with my husband, and panicked that my child isn't coping at school. But I have now got to a point where I have constructed a life that limits or eradicates my misery triggers and embraces and enhances the things that bring me joy.

As the wise voices I shared above suggest, I've found that happiness really does come from within, not from a holiday, money or a compliment. These can give you a thrill – certainly – but the baseline of joy needs to be less fleeting and more grounded within your heart or head than a brief piggyback to pleasure.

The scientifically proven bringers of bliss

Research published in the *World Leisure Journal* highlighted, when studying 751 British families, how the best predictor of familial happiness came when quality leisure time was valued in the home, with members focusing on routines they could do together. I was relieved to read this study. I feared that I was becoming incredibly boring and turning my children and husband the same way. We'd got into a rut – film and pizza night on Fridays, soccer games on Sundays, Harry Potter reading every night in January – but we all thrived on it, looking forward to these traditions and a certain sequence of events. To understand that family rituals increase security and contentment, and with that happiness, was a great relief and it helped me to understand our need for routine.

Being kind to others releases the feel-good hormone serotonin, so do a good deed. According to a study on happiness from the University of British Columbia, helping others can reduce social anxiety and boost joy, alertness and interest in life for up to four weeks. Helping out at my son's school or listening to a friend when she needs a shoulder to cry on is doing me as much good as it does them, it turns out.

Increasingly, as a mother, I feel the need for silent contemplation Be it meditation, yoga, a quiet bath with my thoughts or ten minutes lying on the grass in my back garden looking at the sky, they all give me a trance-like feeling when I can let fears wash in and wash out. The *Journal of Science and Healing* reveals how meditation can alleviate an individual's stress and suffering, improving their psychological state and their quality of life. If *I* felt it, I pondered a year ago, would my children too? They began to enjoy app-led five-minute meditations with me, and I encouraged them to colour and draw more too – quiet pastimes that allow the brain to unwind and wander more than more frenetic leisure activities.

I refuse to swallow my sadness Hiding my frustrations and emotions makes them worse. I've learnt to share, ask for help and solve issues head-on rather than trying to bury them. The National Institute of Mental Health advise 'talk therapy' or counselling as a great way to start healing your way to happiness, and if that is not available, simply spending time and confiding in people in whom you trust to help you find solutions is invaluable.

A 2016 study by the University of Colorado showed a direct correlation between exercise and the psychological uplift in women's mood. Don't I know it? I'm not a gym bunny, but I do know that the boost of endorphins I get from marching 6,000 steps with a friend after school drop-off, getting fresh air and vitamin D, shifts me from a low to a high frequency. I know that a family disco in the living room reduces the stress hormone cortisol that's rushing around my flustered bloodstream and dampens my children's bad moods or sad slumps. A hike in the woods or a walk on the beach only doubles the bliss, a connection with nature being a guaranteed glee-giver, according to *Frontiers in Psychology*.

The *Journal of Sleep Research* studied women for two weeks and found a direct correlation between good-quality sleep and greater happiness, formulating what every tired mama knows: sufficient shut-eye wards off depression and anxiety. I've learnt that sleep has to be a priority, and that fewer than seven hours a night makes me grumpy and every molehill becomes a mountain. I've learnt that a bedtime routine that includes an aromatherapeutic bath or hot shower, a snuggle and book with my kids, a bubblegum television comedy instead of a depressing news show, and comfy, cotton pyjamas brings me cheap-and-easy elation. I value these nights more than the hectic, high-energy, high-drama nights out of my pre-kid years.

Kids make it harder to be happy!

A 2016 study on the effects of parenting on an adult's happiness published in the *American Journal of Sociology* discovered that parenting can be a mixed blessing for couples, bringing greater anxiety, depression and marriage dissatisfaction than their peers without children. This was especially true for parents in Great Britain, Australia and the United States, and it was linked to the disruption of work–life balance and feeling unsupported by their government's social policy. Know, therefore, that you are not alone, and give yourself a break. Parenting is *officially* hard.

Your Week of Wonder: Hit your peak each day of the week

Embrace the routine of parenting by setting yourself daily check-ins, check-ups and check-outs. You won't mind the day-to-day grind (so much!) when you're committed to making a little room in your diary just for you. Set a reminder along with your morning alarm to create a sequence that allows you to wake up and do, rather than wakeup and drift. These daily mantras will soon become rituals, breaking bad habits or the self-neglect you've been functioning under, and helping you to reach goals, create structure and save time.

Monday
Make-a-move Monday: start your week by putting your best foot forward. Take a stroll when you'd normally take the car; call your friend while you're doing laps of your garden, instead of sitting on the sofa; enroll in a weekly Zumba class with your energetic neighbour. Feel good endorphins will trigger a rush of self-esteem and energy, improve sleep and lower anxiety and blood pressure ... all good for people who can do without a manic Monday.

Tuesday
Turn-it-up Tuesday: make listening to your favourite music a priority today: in the car, in the shower, while you're rushing from home to the office. Charles Darwin once said, 'If I had my life to live over again, I would have made a rule to read some poetry and listen to some music at least once a week' – and you know how smart he was. Don't delay, bring it on today. You shouldn't live with any Darwinian regret, and listening to music boosts mood, mental alertness and memory.

Wednesday
Wind-down Wednesday: relaxation allows our bodies and minds to recover from the barrage of appointments, commitments and fulfilments we throw at ourselves all week. 'Hump Day' is the perfect midway marker to take your foot off the pedal and find an hour to meditate, take a stroll through nature, read a book, watch a movie, socialise with low drama comrades. If you can't escape the kids midweek, bring them into your chillout circle with you, teaching them simple yoga moves or reading a book together.

Thursday

Thirsty Thursday: check in with how you've cared for your physical body so far this week. Have you been drinking enough water? Not overdoing the coffee, fizzy drinks or alcohol? Think of easy ways to boost your H2O levels ... keep flavoured water in the fridge, keep a bottle in the car, make it your mission to take a rehydrating swig every hour. Hydration reduces fatigue, aids weight loss, prevents headaches and eases constipation. Water for the win!

Friday

Free day, fun day, Friday: let loose and live a little – the weekend starts now! Make it your mission to do something for no other reason that it will make you laugh. Go dancing, watch a stand-up comic, have a cocktail with your best friend, take your dog for a long walk, bunk off work an hour early for a sneaky date with your partner. Having fun is a foolproof way to reduce cortisol levels, boost serotonin and improve our everyday ability to cope with what the world throws at us.

Saturday

Solo Saturday: seek out an hour – or more if you can – for some alone time over your weekend. Solitude not only gives you a much-needed break from the constant noise of motherhood but will give you a chance to get ahead. Solitude sparks creativity (oh the chance to daydream without interruptions!) and allows your brain to check in with its plans and ideas, and what you want to change going forward. Quiet time allows you to get to know yourself better – a must-have for a Zen mama.

Sunday

Self-compassion Sunday: reward yourself for a week well-lived and a family well-managed by treating yourself to something that fills your cup and lifts your mood. A yoga class, a spiritual service, a walk in the woods, a home-cooked roast dinner, a family matinee on the sofa with Walt Disney ... Before the hamster wheel starts revolving again, make a space for a slowdown that smooths out the fraught edges of modern motherhood and allows you to be still.

Mama says: Nicola, 40

'It took my divorce to figure out how to balance my work as a lawyer with motherhood. When I was married, I was frantic to be around them whenever I wasn't working, but my time with them reeked of a frenetic energy as I tried to fit too much "fun" into the time we had. Now I only have my kids half the time, our interactions are much more meaningful and substantive. At the risk of sounding trite, it is about quality and not quantity. I save errands and late meetings for the days I don't have them, and get ample me-time then, too. As a result, I am a happier person when I see them. When we are together, I don't feel the need to over-schedule, but I go with the flow, our moods and the weather. When they stay with me, I am really there with them. We chat about school over Play-Doh, have dance-offs, and slumber parties in my king-sized bed. We might stay in pyjamas all day. I'm more in touch with what we each need to be happy that day.'

How can we help our kids to be happy?

What does a child need to be happy? Every child is different, with different needs, and facing unique circumstances, people and events. One of my children thrives on one-to-one time and conversation, the other is super social and longs for adventure. But scientists and researchers agree that there are a few things that parents can do to ease their child's journey from fraught to fulfilled:

1. **Make your family motto** 'effort, not perfection'. Praise their diligence and determination not their natural ability or gold medals. This will make children engage in the process and stop worrying about pleasing you or disappointing you. Don't negatively compare them to their siblings or friends.

2. **Encourage them to foster** strong, meaningful relationships, and lead by example. Perform small acts of kindness together, timetable free time at the park with friends, talk to them about the value you place on good family and friends.

3. **They need *you* to be happy!** Parents with low moods can cause behavioural problems in children, so before you worry about anyone else, you need to take care of your emotional and physical needs. This isn't selfish – extensive research has proven a link between mothers who suffer with depression and negative outcomes for their children.

4. **Always look on the bright side of life** Use your sad moments or disappointing outcomes – and theirs – as teaching moments, to set their brain at a place from where they can look at a glass as half-full rather than half-empty. Teaching optimism, research shows, reduces depression in teenagers and hands them a knack for positivity that they will take into adulthood. Alongside this, however, don't brush off negative emotions: teaching your child to label their feelings while you validate them is key to building their emotional intelligence. They should feel heard and understood, even while you teach them that bad behaviour is not acceptable.

5. **Teaching a child self-discipline** will help them to regulate their lives, follow good patterns and make healthy choices, all of which lead to happiness. It will also boost their confidence and ability to be alone. Willpower predicts success even better than

intelligence, another route to happiness, so teach your children how to plan ahead (lead by example), reward healthy behaviour and never skip breakfast, which research proves promotes good behaviour and the ability to follow rules.

Child's play versus the pressure to be perfect

The playwright Tom Stoppard wrote, 'Because children grow up, we think a child's purpose is to grow up. But a child's purpose is to be a child.' Once we remember that, a lot of the annoyances we find ourselves struggling with as mothers can float away – and with that the clashing moments of yelling, telling off or disappointment that reduce both a parent and child's happiness. We too often consider the words and actions of our children as if they were on our level, with our years of conditioning, experiences and brain development. They are not. They are remarkable little creatures learning to find their way in the new world, so if they have a meltdown when they can't untie their shoelaces, or they spill their juice as often as they manage to drink it, or moan about practising their violin when they were the ones who begged to learn, we have to remember that they are getting to grips with the globe.

If we take the pressure off them to always be better, to be perfect, to compete and to learn, think how much happier they could be? Their main responsibilities are to grow. Your main responsibility is to keep them safe, healthy and as happy as possible. There is a current trend for 'intensive parenting', where mums and dads add pressure to their child's plate with a packed schedule of extracurricular activities, tutoring, competitive sports and academic superiority. These are all heavily timetabled and overseen by anxious parents – and they can even start from babyhood, booking them in for story time, swimming and baby-drumming circles – but these activities can leave children exhausted, fearful of failure and unable to be self-reliant. Recent studies also show this upbringing can lead to an increase in depression and dissatisfaction later in life. For you, mama, it's not great news either – this intense trend of being the perfect parent to the perfect child increases your fear for your child's future and decreases your confidence that you are doing a good enough job.

You know what you have to do, right? And it's free and easy, much simpler and cheaper than overloading your family life with lessons, games and classes. You have to let your children play. Let them be free. Let them use their imagination. Let them live in the moment. Love them with logic. Sadly, over the last two decades children have been losing their unstructured, spontaneous playtimes to structured, instructor-led regimes, and our kids' emotional, social and physical needs are suffering, as are our bank balances and social anxiety. Playing with their peers allows children to negotiate, speak up for themselves, find courage and resolve conflicts. And don't feel guilty if you work and simply can't fit in play dates. Playing with family in an easy-breezy way is a major booster, too. Consider play time as important as piano lessons – or more so!

Is my family *entitled* to be happy?

Open any newspaper or catch a documentary on the BBC, and the horror, violence and poverty faced by much of the globe can make us feel awkward, unworthy and unjustifiably blessed. With access to clean water, fresh food, a healthcare system and an education we are in an exalted position. Yet still, too often, we find ourselves jealously comparing ourselves to those who have more *stuff*! We feel entitled to *more stuff*! And our children can be the worst at this. But in pursuit of happiness, we need to count our blessings. An essay by the Harvard Medical School tells us how feeling gratitude makes you happier, because it reminds you to acknowledge the goodness in your life rather than filling your head with the negatives. You are not owed anything. You are lucky. Be grateful. If anything, you have too much stuff!

My mother, a single mother working three jobs for a chunk of my childhood, taught me the value of things. She said no to churlish demands, made me save for things that I wanted (I still treasure the memory of my first pair of Reebok trainers, hard earned aged 16 from Saturday job earnings accrued over three months) and made sure that I appreciated others' generosity – be it their time or a gift. I am determined to pass this on to my children, which is hard in this era of too much, too quickly, too easily. Some friends buy their children anything they want, when they want it; my two (and they feel I am very cruel) are told to 'add it to their Christmas list' – even in July. When they receive a gift, they send a thank-you video or message, and we chat about how someone had to spend their hard-earned money and limited time making it happen. Because we limit our own gift-giving and they understand others' sacrifices, they appreciate everything and gifts get used and adored.

The fun in forgiveness

Whenever I am confronted with someone else's drama, I am thankful that I am not dealing with it. Now, instead of feeling personally assaulted, offended or humiliated if I or my child is not included in an event, or a work contact doesn't reply to my email, or someone lets a door swing in my face as I'm exiting a coffee shop, I see the bigger picture. This isn't about me, so

I forgive them. Living with an attitude of forgiveness lowers blood pressure, heart rate and cortisol and it reduces the sensation of pain, which in turn make us happier. People are going through all kinds of dramas and upset and are just trying to get through their day. Don't allow them to make you feel unhappy or annoyed; use the moment to feel grateful that you are having a better or calmer day.

Building family rituals

Life is tough. The day-to-day grind can exhaust our bones and drain our positivity. It's important, therefore, to create and nurture tiny slithers of magic and marvel, and bring them into our routines and homes. Borrow some of these bliss-bringers that suit your brood:

- On New Year's Day, decorate an empty jar and leave it somewhere everyone can see it. Fill it with notes from each family member as the year progresses, celebrating successes and moments – a new puppy, a good grade, a joke you all loved, a compliment from a friend – then tip it out and read them aloud on New Year's Eve. It's amazing what small but gorgeous moments and events you'll have forgotten.
- Instead of the Tooth Fairy just leaving a coin or a note under the pillow, amp up the wonder by asking *her* to decorate the gift in green glitter. A friend had another great idea for if you have a messy child: leave a note from the Tooth Fairy with the money explaining how she nearly tripped over toys that were all over the floor while delivering the cash and that she'd love it if the floor was tidied up for her future visits. It works a treat – and makes vacuuming a lot easier, apparently.

- On the first day of spring, plant seeds in a pot or in the garden. Watch them grow and bloom. On the first day of summer, draw or note their beauty and growth. Measure yourselves on the first and last day you do this ritual, too, to see how much you have grown and bloomed.
- Make a vision board that all family members can add to: include things that you want to read, watch, places you want to go to, things you want to build. Work out as a family how you can make these things happen.
- At the end of the day or the week, have a negative knockout: share niggles that have been bothering you in the group, work out why it upset you, forge a plan if it should happen again, then say bye-bye. Make your arms and your home a safe space. Children will behave 900 per cent worse for you than their teachers, neighbours or friends, because you are the bin in which they can throw all their rubbish. Show your kids how you take control of your mind and work out what matters. Don't let negative thoughts rule your roost.
- Make an art gallery space in your home where their creativity and hard work is clearly appreciated, and you can keep track of their improvements and ideas. It doesn't seem like a big deal but it will subconsciously teach your child that what they create matters.
- Keep a list of family rules and mottos that you decide democratically – it'll make your kids feel their opinions are heard. Our list includes a variety of things from not riding motorbikes to always offering a guest a drink in the first ten minutes of them coming into our home.
- Pick a family theme song. Change it regularly. Dance to it, introduce it to friends, play it at home and in the car. Go through the eras together – from your childhood tunes to the latest hits. Check out the joyful list on page 210.

- Celebrate and nurture your children's, and your, natural talents. Don't push your dreams on your offspring; get excited by their dreams.

- Mark historic or cultural landmarks with pomp and circumstance and a bit of pizazz: a royal wedding or baby, Guy Fawkes Night, Day of the Dead, an election where you can take your kids to the polling station with you when you vote – these events give you a chance to teach your children about their family history and the history of their country, while thinking up new ways to remember the significance of the event.

- Treasure special family moments with trinkets. Buy a fridge magnet or Christmas decoration when you go on holiday. They'll bring back happy, inexpensive glee every time they catch the eye or you hang them on the tree. Check in with memories of magic moments on a regular basis to keep them alive.

- Own your family deal breakers. Accept your finicky foibles (mine are good manners and kindness – tidiness not so much). Clearly set out your family values and avoid the 'because I said so' style of discipline. Explain how their words or actions, or *your* words or actions, can make other people feel. Explain the consequences.

- Reminisce about your life pre-children. Remember when you wanted what you currently have: the label of 'mother', a busy lap, the feeling of unconditional love, miniature jokers who think the world of you. Be happy.

- A smart grandmother said to me recently, 'If you want your kids to be happy and self-sufficient, spend half as much money on them, but spend twice as much time with them.' I think this can be a good reminder for all parents, when we are tempted to value material things we can buy our children over the emotional things we can give them.

Happy feet

Ten songs to fill your family with joy:

'Don't Stop Me Now' by Queen

'Best Day of My Life' by American Authors

'MMMBop' by Hanson

'I Lived' by OneRepublic

'The Edge of Heaven' by Wham!

'Can't Stop the Feeling' by Justin Timberlake

'A Cover is Not the Book' by Lin-Manuel Miranda and Emily Blunt

'Party in the USA' by Miley Cyrus

'Wonderful Life' by Zendaya

'Happier' by Marshmellow featuring Bastille

Mama says: Rachel, 35

'Every night we have family dinners – a valued tradition (mostly by me). The dinners are often hectic, loud, gross (burping, farting, spitting), but sitting together is important to me. Every couple of weeks we have a "picnic". If the weather is nice, we eat dinner outside, if it's not, we just lay out a blanket and eat on the living room floor. We also have "opposite nights" when we wear our shirts backwards, sit under the table, and eat dessert before dinner. A mess is usually made, but I love these nights.'

When life gives you lemons . . .

. . . make your own homemade, family-style lemonade. Finding custom routes to self-care and tenderness can make bad times better. Set up a physical or mental closet of family comforters you can always turn to: slippers by the front door, a homemade soup recipe, a particular brand of bath bomb, a poem, a bench in the local park. When our house is knocked down by flu or sickness, we follow default steps that are code for getting better soon and resting up: we drink Lucozade (a treat which is banned at all other times), take in a *Grand Designs* marathon, read Madeline books and scoff salt and vinegar crisps. These tiny gestures have become shorthand for making tough times a bit easier, and I'm sure my kids will be cooing for a Kevin McCloud voiceover to their illness even in their forties. Bad weather is not a bad thing, but it gives us the opportunity to take resting and hibernating to a new level: we make nests out of cushions and duvets on the living-room floor and play Monopoly. If one of us has received some sad news or is feeling a little discombobulated, we watch pop videos and take it in turns to jump into an oily lavender and peppermint bath. Seek those bolstering pleasures that will soothe your family through rocky patches.

So happy together – and alone

There is no one-size-fits-all mode of happiness – the cookie cutter variety rarely works long term. If you love something, expose your kids to it, but don't feel bad, sad or mad if they aren't as into it as you are. I love bunnies, and whenever we go to a petting zoo or a friend's house with rabbits, I try to get my two to show as much enthusiasm for the furry friends as I feel. 'No thanks, mama,' Matilda always says, 'I don't want to get my hands dirty.' I can't understand her! I'm offering fluffy fun and she is rejecting it? How? Because she's more interested in the cake being offered indoors, or introducing herself to the new kid. And that is fine. She is not wrong or weird: she is Matilda. Do share your passions and excitement with your kids – often they'll see the joy you get and be thrilled to connect with you over it – but don't force it. Forced fun is fake fun.

A recipe for success

A friend of mine, who is a family lawyer and relationship counsellor, shares this message with her friends and clients every festive season: Holly's recipe for happiness. I've tasted it and it's delicious.

1 tbsp of Patience

1 tbsp of Cooperation

1 tbsp of Letting Go of Perfection

1 tbsp of Living in the Moment

the zest of Not Comparing Your Family to Other Families

a splash of Gratitude

Mix it all up in a bowl called Love and bake at whatever your definition of Family is – and always (keep your) cool before serving.

Mama says: Louise, 40

'Playing hide-and-seek has been a sanity saver. I'm connecting with my kids yet I'm getting some peace and quiet all by myself in a cupboard. I've realised that my kids' happiness comes from simple, inexpensive engagements like this, or reading together, being outdoors or playing board games. I'm a recovering perfectionist and there have been so many moments as a mother when I've had to step back and remember: "Wait, I didn't do/have X, Y, Z in my childhood and I had a happy life. Why do I think I need to set it all up perfectly for my kids?" I used to punish myself for not playing with them constantly, but in the last few years I've realised how harshly I've been judging myself and I've reeled in my expectations and adjusted my parameters of what a "good mum" is and does.'

Political parties

Nothing brings joy like a party, right? Well, yes, before you became a parent. As a mama, blowing out candles on a cake has become bipartisan. Other mothers often ask if my child has been invited to something, and I can tell from their glum face that their child has not. If mine has had the invitation, I'll explain why to give perspective and soften the blow ('They live in our street too', 'They play in the same soccer team', 'They probably feel they have to because we invited them to a party'). If they haven't, and I like the mum and child and I have the time, I ask if she wants to plan a play date so that our kids will be having fun too and feel less alone or left out. I also remember, and I remind them if appropriate, that parties are expensive and limits have to be set, and that a three-hour stint of screaming and cold pizza in a jumpy house does not bring long-lasting happiness.

When throwing a party, I try to invite the whole class, if it's a small class (invitations are thrown out around the playground as bribes and ammunition so all the children will know about the event), or keep it very small and structured. A good idea is to match the number of kids with the age your child is turning; for example, five friends for a fifth birthday. And remember to only do what you can afford and mentally handle. Kids will usually say that they want a huge, extravagant affair, but when the day arrives, they'll be happy surrounded by love as the centre of attention, in their home, being a little wilder than usual. Do not ruin your birthday with anxiety over party bags, baking from scratch, cleaning your bathrooms, and fulfilling every want on a birthday wish list. You need time to reflect on what a happy day this is for you too, mummy!

Your PG rating

Meditate on the words below, and note your thoughts and ideas on how to make them work for you and your family.

The Ps:

Purpose To learn to be happy with what you have and to teach your family to do the same.

Perspective What do you and your family enjoy/want more of/rejoice in? Shift your perspective to a position of gratitude rather than one of longing or lacking.

Presence Boost your chance of bliss right now: call a friend, go outside, pay someone a compliment, turn off your social media, take a nap, hug your kids, forgive yourself for an earlier mishap, dance up a storm.

The Gs:

Gratitude Being happy doesn't mean that everything is neat and perfect, it means looking beyond the imperfections. Be thankful for the things that make you feel joy, peace and elation.

Goals To begin rituals, routines and pastimes that will increase your family's happiness.

Going for it Acknowledge the sad and difficult times you've had, thank them for the lessons they taught you, then stop waiting for happiness to find you – delve inside yourself and find it.

TAKE A DEEP BREATH, MAMA

Everyone has a unique road to happiness. Drive on yours, not anyone else's – and don't be tricked by warning signs or beeping, or distracted by the lights or shinier cars speeding past. Authentic happiness comes from the small moments of bliss – the laughter, the softness, the completeness – you feel when you connect with your true self and your loved ones. Appreciate those moments, and store them away in your heart to remember forever.

Epilogue – Peace Out

Now that you've come to the end of *The Zen Mama*, I hope you feel more able to denounce the rules and regulations that onlookers, or society, or social media, have tried to impose on your family – those exterior commands that don't bring you contentment or joy. (I do, however, very much encourage you to re-read and make notes on the PG Ratings sections when new worries or triumphs enter your head or your life.)

I hope you trust yourself more, that you feel confident enough to ban the superfluous noise and drama from your family life, and rather than wasting time worrying about what other people think about your choices that you are able to stand tall and breathe deeply.

I hope you are living in the moment more, with an attitude of gratitude, celebrating the people you value and who value you, that you're no longer comparing yourself to others, a bad habit, which doesn't do anyone any good.

You're still going to have a million hard moments. I mean, that's a mother's lot. It's because you care, you hope, you fight, you grow, you bond, you hurt, you envy, you fail, you regret, you change. And that's okay, because you're a mama, but you're also a human being. During these tough times, you need to remember that a moment will not last forever, and if you need to give yourself a break, take it. Remember what I wrote in the introduction: self-care and self-compassion are crucial, to you and your family.

Everyone will survive if you decide not to leave the house one Sunday because you feel sad, or you drive your kids to school in your pyjamas because you're tired, or you order pizza two nights in a row because you're busy, or you let your children miss baths for a week because you haven't got the patience to deal with their moaning. In the grand scheme of your lives together, these things do not matter. They won't even be remembered.

What does matter is the overall vibe of your family, and I know that you're going to find bliss after reading this book and being brave and honest enough to think about your motherhood journey and the changes and choices you can make so that it becomes what you want and need it to be.

You are Zen because you know what values are important to your family and what values are not important to your family.

You are Zen because you know what your purpose as a parent is and what your family's shared goals are.

You are Zen because in accepting the monotony, the reality, the often relentlessness of motherhood, you have grown, and softened, and strengthened, and you are filled with an honest, deeper appreciation for the good things and the good times that you share with your friends, family and community.

I wish you every happiness as you walk, dance, stumble and sway alongside your children on your unique path to Zen. You got this, mama. Namaste.

Further Reading

Books

Brown, Brene, *The Gifts of Imperfection: Let Go of Who You Think You're Supposed to Be and Embrace Who You Are*, Hazelden FIRM, 2010

Gardner, Howard and Katie Davis, *The App Generation: How Today's Youth Navigate Identity, Intimacy, and Imagination in a Digital World*, Yale University Press, 2014

Gurdon, Meghan Cox, *The Enchanted Hour: The Miraculous Power of Reading Aloud in the Age of Distraction*, Piatkus, 2019

Kelby, Scott, *The Book for Guys Who Don't Want Kids*, Peachpit Press, 2005

Louv, Richard, *Last Child in the Woods: Saving our Children from Nature-Deficit Disorder*, Atlantic Books, 2010.

Palmer, Sue, *Toxic Childhood: How the Modern World Is Damaging Our Children and What We Can Do About It*, Orion, 2006

Rich, Adrienne, *Of Woman Born: Motherhood as Experience and Institution*, Norton, 1976

Stadlen, Naomi, *How Mothers Love and How Relationships Are Born*, Piatkus, 2015

Helpful websites

Family life

Coram Family and Childcare: familyandchildcaretrust.org

Dirt is Good - Free the Children: dirtisgood.com

National institute of Play: nifplay.org

Motherhood

La Leche League GB: laleche.org.uk

National Childbirth Trust: nct.org.uk

Postpartum Support International: postpartum.net

Royal College of Midwives: rcm.org.uk

The Motherhood Initiative for Research and Community Involvement: motherhoodinitiative.org

Health

Mental Health UK: mentalhealth-uk.org

NHS England: england.nhs.uk

Public Health England: https://www.gov.uk/government/organisations/public-health-england

Royal College of Paediatrics and Child Health: rcpch.ac.uk

The National Center for Complementary and Integrative Health: nccih.nih.gov

The National Institute of Mental Health: nimh.nih.gov

General

Office for National Statistics: ons.gov.uk

For more on the research included in *The Zen Mama*

Alden, Lynn E. and Jennifer L. Trew, 'Kindness reduces avoidance goals in socially anxious individuals', *Motivation and Emotion*, 39(6): 892 (2015), print

Barr, Sabrina, 'The average Brit checks their phone 10,000 times a year, study finds', Independent.co.uk, 1 December 2017, Web

Bolderdijk J.W. and Y. Joye, 'An exploratory study into the effects of extraordinary nature on emotions, mood, and prosociality', *Frontiers in Psychology* 5:1577 (2015), print

Center on Addiction at Columbia University, 'The importance of family dinners', September 2012, Web

Chung, S. J., A.L. Ersig, and A.M. McCarthy, 'The influence of peers on diet and exercise among adolescents: A systematic review', *Journal of Pediatric Nursing*, 36:44–56 (2017), print

Debrot, Anik, Nathalie Meuwly, et al., 'More than just sex: Affection mediates the association between sexual activity and well-being', *Personality and Social Psychology Bulletin*, (2017), Web

Dunbar, R.I.M., 'Do online social media cut through the constraints that limit the size of offline social networks?', Royal Society Open Science, 1 January 2016, Web

Field, Tiffany, 'American adolescents touch each other less and are more aggressive toward their peers as compared with French adolescents,' *Adolescence*, 34:136 (1999), print

Glass, J., R.W. Simon and M.A. Andersson, 'Parenthood and happiness: Effects of work–family reconciliation policies in 22 OECD countries', *American Journal of Sociology*, 122(3):886–929 (2016), print

Glass, J., R.W. Simon and M.A. Andersson, 'The parenthood "happiness penalty": The effects of social policies in 22 countries', *PRC Research Brief*, 2(7) (2016), print

Hadfield, L., N. Rudoe and J. Sanderson-Mann, 'Motherhood, choice and the British media: A time to reflect', *Gender and Education*, 19(2):255–63 (2007), print

Holt-Lunstad, J., T.B. Smith and J.B. Layton, 'Social relationships and mortality risk: A meta-analytic review', *PLoS Med*, 7(7) (2010), print

Kalmback, David A., Vivek Pillai, et al., 'The interplay between daily affect and sleep: A 2-week study of young women', *Journal of Sleep Research*, 23(6) (2014), print

Klein, Sarah, 'Eight reasons to make time for family dinner: Research from Brigham Young University study,' Health.com, 2 March 2016, Web

Kuo, F.E. and A.F. Taylor, 'A potential natural treatment for attention-deficit/hyperactivity disorder: Evidence from a national study', *American Journal of Public Health*, 94(9):1580–6 (2004), print

Mackenzie, Jean, 'The mothers who regret having children', bbc.co.uk, 3 April 2018, Web

Malhotra, R., M. Stroo, et al., 'The effect of the home environment on physical activity and dietary intake in preschool children,' *International Journal of Obesity*, 37:1314–21 (2013), print

Melton, Karen K. and Ramon B. Zabriskie, 'In the pursuit of happiness all family leisure is not equal', *World Leisure Journal*, 58(4):311–26 (2016), print

Morarka, Vandita, 'Mothers and mental health', The Health Collective, 29 May 2018, Web

Oatridge, Angela, 'Hemispheric differences in the processing of attachment words', *Journal of Clinical and Experimental Neuropsychology* (2008), Web

Pruthi, Sandhya, et al., 'Friendships: Enrich your life and improve your health', Mayoclinic.org, 28 September 2016, Web

Roskam I., M.-E. Raes and M. Mikolajczak, 'Exhausted parents: Development and preliminary validation of the parental burnout inventory,' *Frontiers in Psychology*, 8:163 (2017), print

Tromholt, Morten, 'The Facebook experiment: Quitting Facebook leads to higher levels of well-being', *Cyberpsychology, Behaviour, and Social Networking*, 19(11) (2016), print

Verghese, J., R.B. Lipton, et al., 'Leisure activities and the risk of dementia in the elderly', *New England Journal of Medicine*, 348(25):2508–16 (2003), print

Zamani Sani, Seyed Hojjat, et al., 'Physical activity and self-esteem: Testing direct and indirect relationships associated with psychological and physical mechanisms', *Neuropsychiatric Disease and Treatment*, 12:2617–25 (2016), print

Acknowledgements

Gratitude is a rejuvenating thing to have in trying times, and I'm lucky to be full of it. I am grateful to people who have popped in and out of my life when I've needed them, or not needed them – teaching me important lessons about who to love, who to trust, and how to grow. I am also grateful to those who continue to stick around, anchoring me and supporting me.

To my mama friends who have shared their experiences throughout this book, and in real life during barmy play dates, frantic coffee mornings and glorious grown-up nights out when we actually get to talk without being pestered for pizza or a piggy-back ride: never stop sharing, never stop caring, never stop telling your truth. I'm lucky to be riding alongside you.

To my non-mama friends: never stop rolling your eyes at me when I start obsessing over school fundraisers or junior league football scores. You're a good sanity saver.

Heartfelt thanks to Jillian Young, my beautiful inside and out editor, Jillian Stewart and the team at Piatkus and Little, Brown, and to my agent Zoe Ross and the team at United Agents, who made working on this book a truly Zen experience. Lynda Nardelli, your captivating illustrations are as wonderful as you are, thank you.

My children have been lucky enough to attend schools whose philosophies have taught me, as a parent, as much as they've taught them as students. I'd like to thank everyone at Highland Presbyterian Church Nursery and Weekday School in Louisville,

Kentucky, which follows a child-led, play-based Reggio Emilia philosophy promoting respect, responsibility and teamwork; the teachers and coaches at Crenshaw Athletic Club in Austin, Texas, whose Palaestra programme builds a child's mental and physical strength and emphasises the mind–body connection; and all the staff at Highland Park Elementary, also in Austin, who lead their students with a social–emotional focus, highlighting the importance of kindness, honesty, community and fortitude alongside academic progress. You inspire my children and me every day.

This book could not have been written without my children, William and Matilda, who taught me how to be a mum, and have stuck with me – I mean, what options do they have? – as I've adapted, laughed, stressed, loved, and cried my way to where I am today, holding it – us! – together with joy, acceptance and appreciation. You two are my everything – but you know that already.